THE DEVELOPMENT OF A CONCEPTUAL FRAMEWORK

The Stimulation for Coherence and Continuous Improvement in Teacher Education

Erskine S. Dottin

University Press of America,® Inc.
Lanham   New York   Oxford

Copyright © 2001 by
University Press of America,® Inc.
4720 Boston Way
Lanham, Maryland 20706

12 Hid's Copse Rd.
Cumnor Hill, Oxford OX2 9JJ

Library of Congress Cataloging-in-Publication Data

Dottin, Erskine S.
The development of a conceptual framework : the stimulation
for coherence and continuous improvement in teacher
education / Erskine S. Dottin.
p.   cm
Includes bibliographical references.
l. Teachers—Training of—United States—Evaluation. I. Title.
LB1715 .D63   2001   370'.71'173—dc21   00-066608 CIP

ISBN 0-7618-1939-8 (pbk. : alk. ppr.)

TO

CINDY and FARRELL

The keepers of my castle

CONTENTS

FOREWORD

Teacher education is a critical component of debates about American education in the 21st century. Calls for increased accountability at the school and classroom levels coupled with threats of an ever-impending teacher shortage have placed teacher education very high on the national agenda. Policymakers, politicians, teachers, and parents all have strong, albeit different, opinions about what a person needs to know to be a good teacher. From many perspectives, teacher education is not a difficult endeavor. It involves identifying the knowledge that is important for teachers to know and teaching that knowledge to teacher candidates.

While accomplishing the task seems simple, in truth, teacher education is a highly complex operation. To identify the knowledge that a person needs to know to be a good teacher, one must first define what a good teacher is. What are the characteristics of a good teacher? Can these characteristics be taught or are they inherent or are they learned on the job? What does a good teacher know? What should a teacher candidate know? Is content knowledge enough or should teacher candidates also learn pedagogical knowledge? Is knowledge all one needs to be a good teacher or are there skills and dispositions that are also necessary? And how is this all connected to the mission and the aim of the teacher education program?

At root, these are all deeply philosophical questions and the answers depend upon one's philosophical understanding of teaching and learning. One's understanding of teaching and learning could be steeped in behaviorism or constructivism. It could be attuned to the work of Vygotsky, or Dewey, or Paulo Freire or Frederick Douglas. The philosophical base of a teacher education program, whatever it may be, provides the rationale for what is taught to perspective teachers.

Given a philosophical base, teacher educators must then articulate learning outcomes. That is, they must indicate what teacher candidates will know and be able to do upon completion of the program. The learning outcomes should be consistent with the program's philosophy, based on current research, and informed by the institutional, state and national standards. Once articulated, the outcomes must be measured to ensure that teacher candidates are indeed learning what the program aims to teach.

The field has moved toward a preference for performance-based measures of teacher candidate learning and program operations. This means that assessments are based on what candidates know and can do and are aligned with learning outcomes. Such assessments can include licensing test scores, assessments of clinical experiences, student teaching videos, portfolios of student work, and surveys of graduates and employers. And to assess the quality of unit operations, inputs such as the qualifications of faculty, the strength of the clinical experience, the resources, are often tied together in evaluations of the unit. Finally, the data gathered as a result of candidate assessment and evaluation of unit operations should be used to improve the programs offered. So, far from being a simple task, teacher education is indeed a highly complex endeavor.

From over 20 years of empirical research, we know that the elements discussed above contribute to a strong teacher education program. The conceptual framework, which is the subject of this book, brings these elements together in a structured and coherent way. The conceptual framework serves as a means for understanding the purposes, learning expectations, and quality assessments of teacher education programs. It is a fundamental component of the National Council for Accreditation of Teacher Education (NCATE) accreditation process and should be a fundamental component of all teacher education programs, regardless of NCATE affiliation.

Inevitably, some who read this book will feel that the conceptual framework tramples on academic freedom, that the coherence that is part of a conceptual framework is antithetical to the eclecticism and multiple knowledge bases so valued in teacher education. Much to the contrary, the book describes the conceptual framework as an overarching structure that allows for a broad range of perspectives but establishes parameters for what the teacher education program believes, values, teaches, and assesses.

This book explains the history of the conceptual framework and discusses its elements in a clear and concise manner. It goes on to pose critical questions that guide teacher educators in the development and/or reassessment of conceptual frameworks. Because it tackles this most important subject in such a comprehensive manner, this book is a major contribution to the literature on teacher education.

Antoinette Mitchell, Associate Director, Accreditation Operations, NCATE

PREFACE

This book represents a conceptual journey for the author. It began with the simple realization that questions of purpose are "why" questions; questions of content are "what" questions; questions of method are "how" questions; and questions of evaluation are "when" questions.

Along the journey, I also came to realize the following, thanks to Robert Fitzgibbons (1981) *Making education decisions: An introduction to philosophy of education:* "in any society, three basic educational issues must be confronted: what should the outcomes of education be? What should be taught? How should it be taught? Decisions regarding the outcomes of education have to do with the point of education. They function to direct our actions by giving them focus as we engage in the process of education. Decisions regarding outcomes establish the framework for subsequent decisions concerning what to teach and how to teach."

I am also grateful to Peter Vaill (1996) *Learning as a way of being: Strategies for survival in a world of permanent white water* for bringing me back in my journey to the idea of systems thinking which suggests we cannot "describe a phenomenon independently of ourselves as perceivers without considering systemic interactions between ourselves and the phenomenon" that is part-whole relationships, and for reminding me that a conceptual framework should supply the kind of vision that will help to lift members of a community and bear them through turbulent and frustrating currents of white water.

ACKNOWLEDGMENTS

Insights for work such as this are not gained in isolation from others. In fact, it is the opportunity to listen to, read others' work, and engage in dialogue with others that forms the incubation framework for one's own ideas and insights. I have, therefore, benefitted in my conceptual journey from listening to persons such as Mary Dietz, Steve Lilly, Lelia Vickers, and Dennis Cartwright; reading the work of persons such as John Dewey, R.E. Fitzgibbons, W.D. Hitt, Kenneth Howey and Nancy Zimpher, James Rath, Gary Galluzzo and Roger Pankratz and Peter Senge; and engaging in dialogue with persons such as Antoinette Mitchell, Donna Gollnick, Carol Smith, Alvin Mahrer, Lynne Miller, I. Ira Goldenberg, Martin Hamburgh, Maria Duque, Gwenith Terry, and the many participants and facilitators in the annual AACTE/NCATE Orientations, and the many participants at the National Council for Accreditation of Teacher Education Board of Examiners training sessions, and more particularly, the members of the NCATE 2000 Standards Committee.

I am particularly moved by my colleagues at Grand Valley State University, Michigan, and Azusa Pacific University, California for their interests in putting into operation conceptual frameworks which mirror the ideas in this book.

While I am the beneficiary of the wonderful thinking of the foregoing persons, and units, the development of the ideas in this work rests on my shoulders. If I have mangled any of the thinking of these persons in my effort to get across my ideas then I ask forgiveness of them.

INTRODUCTION

National accreditation has become "high stakes" for colleges/schools/departments of education across the country. Teacher preparation institutions are being judged on the quality effectiveness of their graduates' performance. This performance is linked to the college/school/department meeting new performance standards being promulgated by the National Council for Accreditation of Teacher Education.

One of the critical components of the standards is a college's ability to articulate and share a conceptual framework that provides direction for curriculum, programs, governance, etc. The idea of conceptual framework, while seen as very important in the teacher professional community,[1] has presented difficulty for many institutions to translate and operationalize. Many institutions are in dire need of a work that would help guide their development of a conceptual framework.

Every School/Department/College of Education, as a conceptual system, has a structure. Structure refers to a framework of related conceptual meanings and their generalizations that explain physical, natural, social and human realities. A conceptual framework, therefore, facilitates the fashioning of a coherent perspective into a unit by relating its parts into a coherent whole.

A conceptual framework is more than a **theme** (a subject or topic of discourse or of artistic representation) or a **model** (a set of plans for a building; a miniature representation of something). Instead, a conceptual framework establishes the purpose (the why) of a unit's efforts in preparing teacher education and school personnel candidates. The literature shows that a key variable in effective programs is "coherence," that is, the extent to which curriculum, instruction, the integration of technology, and assessment and evaluation are aligned to form a coherent whole (Koppich & Knapp, 1998). Effective units and programs provide a conceptual framework (the common vision) that helps candidates to see the usefulness of their entire program, including the integration of field and clinical components and other elements of the professional preparation program.

A conceptual framework enables a unit to articulate and share with its professional community its way of seeing, thinking and being. This way of seeing, thinking and being encapsulates the sense of the unit across all unit programs. In addition, it sets forth the operational manner of the unit regarding what candidates should know (content knowledge) and be able to do (curricular, technological and pedagogical knowledge and skills), and the kinds of assessments and evaluation measures needed to produce the desired results in candidates' performance. A unit's conceptual framework should, therefore, provide a sense of direction for the development and refinement of programs, courses, faculty teaching, research and service, candidates and faculty diversity, and unit accountability.

A conceptual framework enables a School/Department/College of Education to articulate the reasons for its existence: its underlying philosophy, its mission consistent with its institutional mission, its aim, learning outcomes for candidates in its programs that define what they should know and be able to do, and to what they should be disposed, the knowledge base(s) from sound research and best practice on teaching and learning upon which the learning outcomes are grounded, and the means by which the desired results in candidate performance will continuously be assessed and evaluated.

Underlying Components

If units view a conceptual framework as a way of seeing the world, that is, as a unit's frame of reference, then they will recognize the necessity of the unit having to articulate it's underlying beliefs and values, it's **philosophy**. Since philosophy enables one to explore questions of existence, then the unit's conceptual framework should include the reason for its existence, its **aim**. Aims give rise to a unit examining why it is preparing its graduates. As a result, **learning outcomes** should be articulated, through **learning objectives** that enable the unit to know what graduates should know (**understandings/knowledge**), be able to do (**skills**), and to what they should be disposed (**dispositions**). These learning outcomes should be grounded in a **knowledge base**. In other words, why the respective learning outcomes are important for a unit should be justified through the knowledge base for teacher education.

The conceptual framework as a way of seeing, thinking and being thus enables units to move from questions of purpose (why) to questions of content (what) to questions of method (how).

xiv

In other words, in utilizing a conceptual framework, a unit states what is delivered in order to achieve its purpose. Consequently, a unit's assessment and evaluation system would entail its ascertaining whether its graduates were acquiring the learning outcomes, and as a result, would provide an understanding of whether the unit was achieving its overall aim, its purpose.

Coherence and Continuous Improvement

A teacher education unit's way of thinking about its purpose (why) and content (matter) and way of delivering the content (manner) should also engender ways of seeing and thinking about the culture of the unit in terms of candidate and faculty composition (diversity), faculty performance and development (scholarship of the classroom), the unit's will to govern, and the unit's capacity to provide necessary resources and facilities to achieve its aim.

A conceptual framework that enhances seeing and thinking in terms of the whole (the unit), to its parts (departments, programs, projects, committees, and so on), and back to the whole (the college/unit), also facilitates a unit's way of making meaning of its decision making in how it delivers its curriculum, how it attends to its candidates, how it enhances faculty vitality, and how unit accountability is provided. In such a framework, goals planning for the unit is given meaning vis-à-vis what is delivered in order to achieve its aim. This goal focused model leads to a relationship between the unit, its departments and programs, and the products and goals each develops in order to enhance a unified and coherent operation.

The aim of a unit may thus be facilitated by a process of continuous improvement that moves from seeing the big unit picture, to the work of the unit to achieve its big picture goals through its parts (departments, programs, etc.), to the use of the results of the foregoing to effect change.

The use of a conceptual framework by a unit enriches its uniqueness. It also reinforces that while there may be many teacher education units, the ends agreed upon by the profession is the goal. The means to those ends may vary, and it is the use of a conceptual framework that provide units freedom to achieve and contribute to professional agreed upon ends in their own unique manner.

Summary

The use of a conceptual framework enables clear distinctions being made between a conceptual framework as a way of seeing, thinking, and being, and a theme, and a model. A unit theme simply is a statement that represents the unit's desired future and therefore guides the unit's day-to-day activities in order bring focus to some desired ends. A unit model enriches a theme by being a simplified representation of different unit operations. However, the unit's conceptual framework encompasses both theme and model by establishing a sense of unity across all the programs in the unit. It provides a sense of direction for development and refinement of programs, courses, teaching, research and service by faculty. It sets forth the operational manner of the unit, and it establishes goals that will lead to a unified whole while still permitting individual interests and pursuits.

Notes

1. During the open hearings at annual meetings of the Association for Teacher Educators, and the American Association of Colleges for Teacher Education for the NCATE 2000 Standards (1998-1999) the one consistent request that came from the professional community regarding the standards was the call to retain the idea of the conceptual framework in the standards.

CHAPTER ONE

CONCEPTUAL FRAMEWORK: DEFINITIONAL CONSIDERATIONS

A quick perusal of the literature clearly shows that there is no working consensus on the definition of the term conceptual framework. Some authors use the term to imply conceptual framework as theory (Grossman, Smagorinsky & Valencia, 1999). Others use the term to denote a model (Doherty, Kouneski & Erickson, 1996). Some prefer to see the term as "an underlying structure and organization of ideas that constitutes the outline and basic frame which guide a modeler in representing a system in the form of a model" (Page, Griffith & Rother, 1998). In other cases, the term means "a shared set of beliefs and attitudes which serve as the foundation for teacher education programs" (Plymouth State College, 2000) or the vision of teaching which guides aspects of teacher preparation (e.g., induction and student teaching programs) (Colton & Sparks-Langer, 1993).

An argument could be made for the relationship between this lack of definitional clarity and the early rate of failure by institutions in meeting the conceptual framework standard. This conceptual framework standard, according to data shared with NCATE Unit Accreditation Board members in 1999 and 2000, was until recently, among three standards which units failed to meet or exhibited weaknesses consistently (candidate and faculty diversity composition being the other standards).

A conceptual framework, however, should be viewed as analogous to the ideology of a society. Sociologists and anthropologists have shown that societies have a set of beliefs, values and ways of understanding that guide the development of policies and are used by those in the society to explain and justify the society's institutions and social arrangements. Such ideologies may be construed of as interpretive lenses through which experiences in a society are organized.

Applying the ideas of Vaill (1996) to the notion of conceptual framework one might deduce that every unit is composed of countless facts and methods whereby problems are solved, interpretations are made, and of course actions are taken without thinking about it. The idea of conceptual framework, in this context, helps us to understand a unit's culture and should therefore facilitate an understanding of part to whole relationships.

Every unit in teacher education may, therefore, be seen as analogous to a micro society, each with a basic structure of beliefs, values and ways of understanding that explain and justify the social and human realities in the respective teacher education program. A conceptual framework for a unit, therefore, becomes the interpretive lens through which experiences in the unit are organized (curriculum, teaching, candidate and faculty performance, field/clinical experiences, and so on).

A conceptual framework is, therefore, a way of seeing, thinking and being in a unit. In other words, a conceptual framework organizes thought processes in a unit. This way of seeing, thinking, and being should encapsulate the sense of the unit across all unit programs. It should provide a sense of direction for the development and refinement of programs, courses, faculty teaching, research, and service, candidates' performance, and unit accountability. In other words, a unit's conceptual framework should facilitate the fashioning of a coherent perspective into a unit by relating its parts into a coherent pattern or whole.

The conceptual framework as a unit's dominant meta-narrative or meta-schemata should not only contain explanations of and justifications for a unit's operations, that is ways of seeing and thinking about the world of professional education, but should also generate self-renewal possibilities for those involved (faculty, candidates, leadership). In other words, a good conceptual framework will create possibilities for a unit to generate working hypotheses to guide the study of and subsequent renewal of its practices and policies. It is the compass for showing how the unit's operation will make life in the unit better for all involved.

To this end, a conceptual framework may be defined accordingly: **A conceptual framework is an underlying structure or system in a professional education unit that gives conceptual meanings to the unit's operation, and provides direction for programs, courses, teaching, candidate performance, faculty scholarship and service, and unit accountability.**

These conceptual meanings facilitate the fashioning of a coherent perspective into a unit by relating its parts into a coherent whole. The framework, therefore, acts as the stimulation of a unit ethos within which continuous improvement, renewal, and change can occur.

It should be noted that the definition of conceptual framework in the revised NCATE 2000 Standards glossary borrows from the foregoing definition:

> **Conceptual Framework** - An underlying structure in a professional education unit that gives conceptual meanings through an articulated rationale to the unit's operation, and provides direction for programs, courses, teaching, candidate performance, faculty scholarship and service, and unit accountability (NCATE 2000 Standards: May 11, 2000).

CHAPTER TWO

THE CALL FOR A CONCEPTUAL FRAMEWORK IN THE ARENA OF NATIONAL ACCREDITATION

Beginnings

The introduction by the National Council for Accreditation of Teacher Education (NCATE) of the concept of continuing accreditation in the mid 1990s concurrently brought to the fore the idea of **conceptual framework**. This notion of continuing accreditation of education units presupposed certain requisite activities on the part of education units: ongoing planning, evaluation and self-study, change for improvement, being future-oriented, and having a vision that guides the work in the unit (NCATE, 1996).

The guiding concepts for a unit's justification of its operation, prior to the idea of continuing accreditation, were "knowledge base(s)" and "model." These concepts were embedded in the NCATE 1987 standards, in particular Category 1, Knowledge Bases for Professional Education, and Standard I.A: Design of Curriculum:

Knowledge Bases for Professional Education
Standard I.A: Design of Curriculum
The unit ensures that its professional education programs are based on essential knowledge, established and current research findings, and sound professional practice. Each program in the unit reflects a systematic design with an explicitly stated philosophy and objectives. Coherence exists between (1) courses and experiences and (2) purposes and outcomes (NCATE, 1992, 47).

The first criterion of compliance for the standard required that:

(1) The unit ensures that its professional education programs have adopted a model(s) that explicates the purposes, processes, outcomes, and evaluation of the program. The rationales for the model(s) and the knowledge bases that undergird them are clearly stated along with goals, philosophy, and objectives (NCATE, 1992, 47).

The standards glossary offered the following definition for "model":

A model for professional education is a coordinated and articulated system or design for the preparation of professional school personnel that has a knowledge base to support it. A professional education unit might adopt one or more models to undergird its programs. Models might be based on direct instruction, cognitive development, individual differences, cultural diversity, effective schools, behaviorism, etc. they might be based on themes or expected outcomes like teacher as decision maker, reflective teaching, etc. (NCATE, 1992, 65).

This push by NCATE in its redesigned standards of the late 80's and early 90's on a knowledge base was according to Gideonse (1992) clearly a reaction to the teacher education professional community's call for "professional education [to] be strongly grounded in research, scholarship, and the knowledge bases of the profession (257-258).

Of course, this knowledge base quest was also linked to the professional education community's need to prove to its critics that it was indeed a profession and like other professions the teaching profession could also boast of a knowledge base for its practitioners. Hence there emerged a plethora of works articulating knowledge bases in teacher education (Dill, 1990; Houston, 1990; Murray, 1996; Reynolds, 1989; Wittrock, 1986).

An emerging reality from the push for a knowledge base for teacher education programs is captured by David Imig in the foreword to Frank Murray's edited book, *The teacher educator's handbook: building a knowledge base for the preparation of teachers:*

… experience gained from the implementation of accreditation standards on the professional knowledge base has pointed toward an emerging research agenda on the conceptual framework for teacher education programs. Responses by approximately five hundred teacher preparation institutions to the knowledge base standards of the National Council for Accreditation of Teacher Education (NCATE) have raised issues about conceptual coherence within the structure of teacher education across individual program (subject matter) areas; about the connection between faculty capacity and credibility of the knowledge base underlying programs; and about the decision-making process for program design in teacher education units (Murray, 1996, xiv).

In fact, voices like Gideonse (1986) had been promoting the need for guiding images for teaching and teacher education "that has normative status ... to guide ... conceptualization of teaching at its best and at the farthest limits of current possibility (187). Gideonse's argument was that the adoption of a particular image of teacher affects the knowledge base required, the preparation model for teaching, and the selection criteria for future teachers. In other words, he maintained that "no solutions to the puzzle of teacher education will be found; they must be designed" (Gideonse, 1986, 188).

Themes, Metaphors and Models

A concurrent thrust in the literature to the quest for the knowledge base was about orientations, that is, themes or models, that have implications for the design and/or selection of teacher education pedagogies (Zeichner, 1983).

The emerging idea here was that the use of themes, metaphors or models provide some sense of coherence for programs (Grow-Maienza, 1990; Grow-Maienza, 1991; Cooley & Hitch, 1993). However, the need for coherence conflicts with what Gideonse (1986) calls "multiple visions of reality" in teacher education. The question is, should teacher education programs operate from a unique model or from multiple and differing models? To Gideonse (1993), utilizing differing models may precipitate a well-intentioned desire to leave professional issues open. However, he feels that in so doing high costs are paid in maintaining coherence.

Cooley and Hitch (1993) and Grow-Maienza (1996) offer examples of programs in which definition and explication of the programs came about only after examination and consideration of the goals and philosophical foundations of the programs and a consensus on the knowledge base and an articulated unique model for the programs. In other words, the notion is that:

> Faculties will have a better sense of their own programs and a greater chance of having coherent, integrated programs if they first look at the programs and articulate the assumptions underlying them....faculties will need then to articulate the knowledge base they will deliver to their students to meet the objectives of their programs, given the assumptions about what teachers

should know and be able to do and how best they can come by that
knowledge and those skills (Grow-Maienza, 1996, 519).

On the other hand, Donmoyer (1996) suggests that "coherence is, in
fact, possible only if we ignore value differences and include in our
knowledge base the research that shares our values and a priori
conceptions of learning and teaching" (107). He worries that:

> [NCATE] does not consider eclecticism an adequate response to its standard
> that a teacher education program be based on a clearly defined knowledge
> base... NCATE [endorses] the principles of coherence and consistency....
> The focus of most NCATE evaluations with respect to the knowledge base
> standard is not on the adequacy of the knowledge base employed; rather, the
> central question in most instances is whether the articulated knowledge base
> has been implemented throughout the program. A program is normally
> judged, in other words, not primarily on the adequacy of the foundation on
> which it is built but rather on the consistency with which that foundation has
> been implemented. In short, coherence is the operative criterion in making
> accreditation decisions with respect to NCATE's knowledge base standard
> (Donmoyer, 1996, 106-107).

Donmoyer (1996) further asserts:

> To the extent that we take the coherence response seriously and design
> teacher education programs around the principle of consistency, however,
> our programs will not only not prepare teachers to choose among or
> thoughtfully combine rival paradigms and purposes ... but teachers we
> educate will not even be made aware of the existence of different paradigms
> and the differing purposes and values they serve (Donmoyer, 1996, 109).

But does it follow that a coherent teacher education operation will
automatically preclude an understanding of different points of view by
teacher education candidates? Buchmann and Floden (1992) suggest
that the call for coherence in teacher education is a meaningful indictor
of worth only if:

> ... coherence allows for many kinds of connectedness, encompassing logic
> but also associations of ideas and feelings, intimations of resemblance,
> conflicts and tensions, previsagements and imaginative leaps (4).

In other words, according to Buchmann and Floden (1992):

> Educational coherence is found where students can discover *and* establish

relations among various areas of sensibility, knowledge, skill, yet where loose ends remain, inviting a reweaving of beliefs and ties to the unknown (8).

It seems evident that the use of a conceptual framework that includes a model or theme to describe and think about a teacher education program will contribute to a greater sense of wholeness and coherence. Arends and Winitzky (1996) contend:

Thematically driven, conceptually coherent programs, ... , are designed precisely to give teacher candidates the experience of discovering their own patterns, for constructing their own theoretically and ethically defensible understandings about teaching and learning. Consistency is not necessarily miseducative; it depends on how it is done. For example, a program can be designed to consistently require candidates to reflect on their practice in light of child development theory, social justice concerns, the process-product research, and/or their own experiences as learners. This type of consistency would be very different from one that, for example, promulgated one and only one model of classroom management in every course and every field experience. At bottom, these issues remain empirical questions; we do not know the effects of coherence and consistency, however they are operationalized on prospective teachers. We do know, however, that something is amiss with the fragmented nature of current programs, and we would argue that it is premature to critique coherence before it has even been tried (551-552).

Stengel and Tom (1996) indicate that integrative and coherent programs in teacher education are possible if:

The program model or metaphor [is] congruent with the program structure. The stated philosophy and the concepts used to express it [are] evident in student assignments and assessment, faculty interactions, and even course titles. At the same time, experience and coursework should not be so tightly controlled as to misrepresent the complex reality of teaching and learning and limit the possibility of creative response (613-614).

The clarion call for coherence in teacher education was made by Howey and Zimpher when they declared "Conceptually coherent programs enable needed and *shared* faculty leadership to engage in more generative and continuing renewal by underscoring collective roles as well as individual course responsibilities" (Howey & Zimpher, 1989, 242).

Their work on cross-institutional case studies clearly confirmed that a vital condition that enables teacher education programs is coherence and cohesiveness in design.

The call for a conceptual framework in national accreditation standards, while driven by a need for coherence in teacher preparation programs, is not a call for total adherence to a single epistemological or empirical knowledge base. Fenstermacher (1994), for example, warns against putting the power of the state or national accrediting bodies behind "a particular epistemological approach to the teaching of teachers" (332) or any single conception of teaching that does not accord with a well-developed theory of education (331).

The call for a conceptual framework is linked to NCATE's application of its standards to a professional education unit, as a whole, and not to specific programs. The conceptual framework should, therefore, help units to focus on the unit, and to be able to refer to programs to highlight how the unit is carrying out its activities and pursuing its vision, mission, etc.

The call for a conceptual framework in national accreditation is a call for the awareness of the metaphor of umbrella (unit) under which unit activities, that is, program operations, are conducted. The unit may, therefore, conceptualize operations for its initial level programs through one conceptual framework, and the operations for its advanced programs through another framework. On the other hand, a unit may conceptualize the operations of its initial and advanced level programs through a single conceptual framework or umbrella.

In any case, to rephrase Galluzzo and Pankratz (1990) reference to the development of a program model for teacher preparation programs: "whether faculty develop a single comprehensive model [conceptual framework] or a series of models [conceptual frameworks] it is essential they show how professional knowledge acquired in the various program elements becomes integrated as a [candidate] progresses throughout the program " (13).

CHAPTER THREE

BUILDING A CONCEPTUAL FRAMEWORK

The initial activity in the development of a conceptual framework is to understand the basic elements in a conceptual framework. This activity is congruent with the process for seeking initial accreditation for an education unit from NCATE. An element of this process is the submission of nine preconditions, one of which (Precondition #4) requires that "The unit has a framework that establishes the shared vision for a unit's efforts in preparing educators to work in P-12 schools and provide direction for programs, courses, teaching, candidate performance, scholarship, service, and unit accountability" (NCATE, 2000, 2).

An education unit that is seeking initial accreditation must first submit its conceptual framework for review by a Preconditions Audit Committee. This committee is supposed to verify that "the structural elements of the conceptual framework are present" (NCATE, 2000, 2).

Preconditions Elements

Structural Element 1: What the Unit Wants to Become and Is Charged to Do

The first element of a unit's conceptual framework is a description of what the unit wants to become. According to Peterson (1995) this description of a unit's desired future is captured in a vision statement. And as Senge (1990) maintains a learning organization is synonymous with a shared vision.

A unit's desired future may, however, be captured in a theme. A theme may be construed of as "an effective means to communicate the essence of a vision and an easy way for people to remember the vision."

A vision may be stated succinctly in a sentence or two and can often be stated as a theme, for example, "facilitating learning and change within diverse populations and environments." A vision or theme is not a strategic plan since plans contain goals and objectives which tell how and when some aim will be achieved.

While the unit's vision or theme communicates a desired future, the unit's mission statement, describes what the unit is charged to do. A vision or theme is, therefore, not a mission. A mission statement is basically a broad general statement of purpose which specifies a unit's reason(s) for existence and establishes the scope of a unit's activities. A unit's mission statement should in some way be congruent with the mission statement of the institution in which the unit resides.

Structural Element 2:   The Justification for the Lens Through Which the Unit Sees the World of Teaching and Learning

Is there a center from which the unit approaches the life of the teacher and other school personnel preparation? In other words, are there underlying commitments to any set of philosophical, psychological and pedagogical beliefs? Does the unit offer reasons through these commitments for its approach to the life of the teacher and other school personnel preparation?

The second structural element of a conceptual framework is, therefore, the *why* of the unit's efforts - its philosophy. The unit's philosophy should enable one to get a sense of the general underlying beliefs in the unit about reality, truth and knowledge, ethics and values which give meaning to the unit's existence, and which form the bases for critical decisions. A philosophy of education vis-à-vis the unit's philosophy is a set of beliefs about reality, truth and knowledge and ethics and value; about how human beings come to know and learn; and about best pedagogical practices.

This element of the conceptual framework may therefore be construed as the justification for the lens through which the unit sees the world of teaching and learning.

John Dewey maintains that "to have an aim is to act with meaning, not like an automatic machine; it is to *mean* to do something and to perceive the meaning of things in the light of that intent" (Dewey, 1944, 104). The philosophy of the unit thus enables one to understand how the unit uses its underlying beliefs - its philosophy of education - to direct its action in making educational decisions about what to teach and how to teach it through an articulated aim, that is, the unit's reason for existence.

Structural Element 3: The Outcomes and Proficiencies Candidates Must Demonstrate and the Empirical and Theoretical Justification

The third structural element of the conceptual framework should provide an understanding of what candidates should know (knowledge), what they should be able to do (skills), and to what they should be disposed (dispositions). Since aims give rise to results, then this element of the conceptual framework should describe the learning outcomes for candidates - the institutional standards by which candidate learning, including the effect of candidate learning on P-12 student learning/performance, will be assessed.

However, the question regarding why the respective learning outcomes are important for the unit must be justified through the knowledge base literature for teacher education (theories, research, the wisdom of practice, and educational policies). The literature on teacher education clearly shows that there are recognized knowledge base(s) that should influence the preparation of teachers and other school personnel (Houston, 1990; Murray, 1996; Reynolds, 1989; Wittrock, 1986).

Lee Shulman (1987), for example, identified three types of knowledge base(s) for expert teaching: knowledge of the subject to be taught (content knowledge), knowledge of how to take the content and help others understand it (pedagogical-content knowledge), and knowledge of the general variety that includes how to motivate students, how to manage groups of students in a classroom setting, how to design and administer performance assessments, and so on (pedagogical knowledge).

Structural Element 4: The Alignment with Institutional, State and National Standards

The fourth structural element of the conceptual framework addresses the idea of a quality effectiveness continuum in professional education. Quality assurance in a unit should be a matter of being guided by internal outcomes (institutional standards) that are congruent and aligned with state and national standards. These standards include those disseminated by:

(1) the Interstate New Teacher Assessment and Support Consortium,
(2) the National Board for Professional Teaching standards, and
(3) subject specialty standards.

Since the professional education unit is a part of a quality assurance continuum, its way of seeing and thinking, its conceptual framework, must therefore explain its contribution to the authority which governs its existence, the State, and to the profession, as manifested in national standards.

As articulated in the Report of the National Commission on Teaching and America's Future (1996):

> Clearly, if students are to achieve high standards, we can expect no less from their teachers and other educators. The first priority is reaching agreement on what teachers should know and be able to do in order to help students succeed. Unaddressed for decades, this task has recently been completed by three professional bodies, The National Council for Accreditation of Teacher Education (NCATE), the Interstate New Teachers Assessment and Support Consortium (INTASC), and the National Board for Professional Teaching Standards (The National Board). Their combined efforts to set standards for teacher education, beginning teacher licensing, and advanced certification outline a continuum of teacher development throughout the career. These standards offer the most powerful tools we have for reaching and rejuvenating the soul of the profession (Summary Report, What Matters Most: Teaching for America's Future, September 1996, p. 18).

The development of professional accountability in teacher education may therefore be seen as a continuum that links a College of Education (a Unit) responsible for the initial preparation of candidates, to the public authority for its operation, a State, to the induction process for candidates into the field (school sites), to the professional and learned societies that shape what is taken for knowledge in the respective fields (national societies), to the accomplished professional as judged by the National Board for Professional Teaching Standards (NBPTS). The following figure captures the essence of the foregoing:

Conceptual Framework Alignment Link

Unit Outcomes: Institutional Standards		INTASC Principles	State Standards	National Board Standards
Learning Objectives - knowledge - skills - dispositions		Learning Objectives - knowledge - skills - dispositions	Learning Objectives - knowledge - skills - dispositions	Learning Objectives - knowledge - skills - dispositions
Program Outcomes	National Program Standards	Subject Standards	Subject Standards	Subject Standards
- knowledge - skills - dispositions	- knowledge - skills - dispositions	- knowledge - skills - dispositions	- knowledge - skills - dispositions	- knowledge - skills - dispositions

The unit's conceptual framework or meta-narrative thus provides an interpretation of how the unit moves from its performance learning outcomes, that is, its institutional standards, to its aligning these outcomes/institutional standards with performance outcomes promulgated in state and national standards.

Structural Element 5: The System for Unit and Program Effectiveness

The fifth and final structural element of the conceptual framework delineates the results orientation and commitment to continuous improvement in the unit's professional community, in other words, unit and program effectiveness. If the unit is moving conceptually from questions of purpose (why), to questions of content (what), to questions of delivery (how), then the crux of its evaluation system must entail its ascertaining whether graduates are acquiring the learning outcomes, that is, meeting the institutional standards, and as a result, whether it is achieving its overall aim. This element of the conceptual framework therefore provides answers to how the unit is achieving and when the unit has achieved its aim.

This element of the conceptual framework describes the extent to which the aim, and outcomes as conceptually developed and organized, will produce and are actually producing the desired results.

In other words, this element of the conceptual framework should highlight:

(a) the active and meaningful participation of the unit's professional community in evaluative and assessment decisions that directly impact the continuous improvement of its programs.

(b) the system for the assessment and evaluation of candidate performance.

(c) the use of and means to valid and reliable internal and external unit operational data for improvement results and ongoing unit accountability.

The Conceptual Framework and Requisite Unit Activities

The acquisition of national accreditation for professional education units (initial and continuing) from the National Council for Accreditation of Teacher Education necessitates units to design, develop, implement and continuously evaluate their conceptual framework(s). The following unit activities are congruent with the foregoing need.

On the other hand, the following activities are conducive with what Vaill (1996) calls "operative knowledge." That is, these activities may be seen as a means of getting a unit, a complex system, to work in a manner consistent with the design intended by a unit's community. The activities, which follow, therefore, facilitate a unit acting with meaning.

Determining the Unit Vision/Theme

According to Block (1987) "creating a vision forces us to take a stand for a preferred future" (102). The unit's desired future for its initial and advanced programs, that is, its vision/theme should emerge as a result of collaborative dialogue among the faculty and members of its professional community. This collaborative endeavor should be framed by Peter Senge's exhortation that learning organizations are synonymous with shared visions (Senge, 1990). In fact, Michael Fullan contends: "Shared vision is important in the long run, but for it to be effective you have to have something to share. It is not a good idea to borrow someone else's vision" (Fullan, 1993, 13).

There are many activities that are conducive to helping a unit design and develop a vision. One of those activities, as outlined by DuFour and Eaker (1998) may be conducted accordingly. Have each member of the unit write a descriptor of what he/she hopes the unit will become. The descriptor may address initial and advanced preparation levels together or separately. According to Roberts and Smith, (Senge et al., 1994, 208) unit participants may be assisted in this process by asking them to think of the following questions: What would you like to see the unit become? What reputation would it have? What contribution would it make to candidates and its community? What values would it embody? How would people work together?

DuFour and Eaker (1998) further suggest that the unit then be divided into small groups so that the groups might do the following.

Each of these small groups should discuss the desired future descriptors of each group member and capture a statement that best describes the group's collective vision. A committee then collects all of the group statements, and develops a draft of a vision statement based on a common theme in the small group statements. This committee's draft is then shared with the entire faculty, and members of the unit's community for critique, and suggested revisions.

The unit committee then revises its draft vision statement based on the foregoing suggestions and offers a second draft for comment. If the majority accept the draft then the unit may use the vision statement as the design and guide for its operation - the preparation of professional educators. A version of this activity was carried out by professional education unit faculty at California State University - Stanislaus, in the spring of 2000, in that unit's quest for a revised vision/theme and outcomes.

An additional activity for a unit in its design and development of a vision statement is to have each department, related school/college, endorse the common vision statement. In turn, each department and program in the unit can then use the process to develop its own statement for the department and program(s) vis-à-vis what they want to become. Each designed and developed department and program(s) statement must then show its consistency with the unit's vision.

Stephen Covey, author of *The Seven Habits of Highly Effective People: Restoring the Character Ethic* (1990), offers an alternative means to a unit to develop a vision/theme. If one applies his ideas to a unit then the unit would begin the process with the end in mind. That is, the unit might get members of its community to think of its demise and articulate the following: What character would the community member liked to have seen in the unit? What contributions and/or achievements does the community member remember most about the unit? What difference has the unit made in the community member's estimation? The essence of these responses may then be discerned as the unit's desired future.

The outcome of these activities is a unit that is instilled with a sense of direction and destination, that has a target of purpose, and in which there is widespread ownership of that direction. In other words, the unit's vision as translated through a theme, that is a statement used to represent or convey its vision of teaching and learning, becomes the unit's definition of success. DuFour and Eaker maintain that a shared vision:

... motivates and energizes people.
... creates a proactive orientation.
... gives direction to people within the organization.
... establishes specific standards of excellence.
... creates a clear agenda for action (DuFour & Eaker, 1998, 84).

On the other hand, Nanus cautions:

Vision plays an important role ... throughout the organization's entire life cycle.... Sooner or later the time will come when an organization needs redirection or perhaps a complete transformation, and then the first step should always be a new vision, a wake-up call to everyone involved with the organization that fundamental change is needed and is on the way (Nanus, 1992, 9).

The activities in a unit that facilitate the development of a vision/theme should enable the unit to address the following questions:

What does the unit want to become?
What is the vivid picture of the unit by which members would like to be remembered?
Is there a statement that might be used to represent or convey the vision of teaching and learning (the common aspirations, interests, etc.) held in the unit?
What meanings are conveyed in the key concepts in the statement vis-à-vis the role of the teacher/professional educator, the unit, and/or the unit's professional community?
Is there any support in the professional literature for the meaning(s) or metaphor(s) conveyed in the theme?

Articulating the Unit Mission

DuFour and Eaker (1998) maintain that:

The mission question challenges members of a group to reflect on the fundamental purpose of the organization, the very reason for its existence. The question asks, 'Why do we exist?' "What are we here to do together?' and 'What is the business of our business?' The focus is not on how the group can do what it is currently doing better or faster, but rather on why it is doing it in the first place. Addressing this question is the first step in clarifying priorities and giving direction to everyone in the organization (58).

While the unit's vision of teaching and learning provides a sense of the unit's desired future, its mission delineates the specific task with which it is charged and offers its <u>raison d'etre</u>, its sense of purpose. In its development of a mission, a unit can direct its activity to two areas (a) tradition within the academy, and (b) state directives for colleges of education.

Tradition in universities, of which colleges of education are a part, calls for a strong commitment to excellence in teaching, research, and service. A unit's translation of its interpretation of its commitment to excellence in teaching, research, and service should therefore be delineated in its purpose, its mission. A unit may, therefore, examine its university's traditional commitment to excellence in teaching, research, and service and develop its own special meaning, identity and sense of itself as a professional community vis-à-vis its commitment to excellence in teaching, research, and service. The need to enhance scholarship is a part of a unit's mission.

On the other hand, historical state directives have charged colleges of education to educate and prepare teachers, administrators, and other school personnel to function as competent, creative, and knowledgeable facilitators of learning, leadership, etc. A unit may also look to its state directive for direction in its development of a mission statement.

The unit's activity in this area of mission development should provide answers to the following questions:

What is the specific task with which the unit is charged?
Why does the unit exist?
What is the unit's institutional purpose?

Building the Unit Philosophy and Aim

If the unit's vision/theme is thought of as the first creation in the development of a conceptual framework, then the values and principles upon which the unit's being and doing will be based may be seen as the second creation, that is, the road map to coherent construction of the framework. Here the unit begins to delineate the basis for its decisions and consequently begins to give meaning to its professional world through philosophical lens. As a result, the unit's philosophical lens provides an underlying aim for its conceptualization of teaching and learning, knowledge and truth, and learning outcomes vis-a-vis institutional standards.

John Dewey noted that philosophy implies "a certain totality, generality, and ultimateness," and "is the endeavor to attain as unified, consistent, and complete an outlook upon experience as is possible" (Dewey, 1944, 324). Dewey further noted:

This direct and intimate connection of philosophy with an outlook upon life obviously differentiates philosophy from science. Particular facts and laws of science evidently influence conduct. They suggest things to do and not do, and provide means of execution. When science denotes not simply a report of the particular facts discovered about the world but a *general attitude* toward it - as distinct from special things to do - it merges into philosophy. For an underlying disposition represents an attitude not to this and that thing nor even to the aggregate of known things, but to the considerations which govern conduct (Dewey, 1944, 324-325).

If Dewey is correct, then units are delineating their general outlook upon life in teacher education in which there is a large faculty commitment to the underlying tenets of that outlook and through which the unit evinces "certain distinctive modes of [professional] conduct" (Dewey, 1944, 324). This normative outlook challenges members in a unit to escape the immediacy of "how" and move to underlying values and principles vis-à-vis "the why."

To determine faculty commitment to the underlying tenets of the unit's general outlook on life in teacher education, some institutions have administered to its faculty an educational or philosophical beliefs inventory. The commitments held in common by the majority of faculty on the inventory are then used as the basis for describing the unit's philosophy.

On the other hand, units may want to adopt and adapt for the unit any of the strategies promulgated as being helpful in enhancing the development of a personal philosophy statement. The unit's activity to delineate its philosophy should enable it to provide answers to the following:

Does the vision/theme and mission suggest underlying commitments to any particular philosophical, psychological, or pedagogical beliefs? Are there any general underlying beliefs about reality, truth and knowledge, ethics and values that give meaning to the unit's existence and/or that form the bases for critical decisions, that is, the center from which the unit approaches the life of teacher and other school personnel preparation?

According to Dewey (1944), an "... aim ... is experimental, and hence constantly growing as it is tested in action" (105):

The aim as it first emerges is a mere tentative sketch. The act of striving to realize its worth. If it suffices to direct activity successfully, nothing more is required, since its whole function is to set a mark in advance; and at times a mere hint may suffice. But usually--at least in complicated situations--acting upon it brings to light conditions which had been overlooked. This calls for revision of the original aim; it has to be added to and subtracted from (Dewey, 1944, 104).

According to the foregoing, a unit's conceptual framework, in particular the unit's aim or purpose, acts as the stimulation of a unit ethos within which continuous improvement, renewal, and change can occur. Units technically do not have aims. It is the collective persons in the unit that have aims. Therefore, as Dewey points out an aim is not an abstract idea but "... is of value so far as it assists observation, choice, and planning in carrying on activity from moment to moment and hour to hour (Dewey, 1944, 107). Dewey further notes that:

To have a mind to do a thing is to foresee a future possibility [vision]; it is to have a plan for its accomplishment; it is to note the means which make the plan capable of execution and the obstructions in the way, --or, if it is really a *mind* to do the thing and not a vague aspiration--it is to have a plan which takes account of resources and difficulties. Mind is capacity to refer present conditions to future results, and future consequences to present conditions. And these traits are just what is meant by having an aim or a purpose (Dewey, 1944, 103).

The unit's activity to articulate its educational aim should enable it to respond to the following questions:

Is there a statement that captures the directing of effort by the unit toward some end?
Does the unit have a clearly directed purpose?
Does this aim emerge from the vision/theme, mission statement and philosophy statement?
Does the aim establish a basis for subsequent decisions about what candidates and other school personnel should know and be able to do, that is, commitments to candidate learning and long-term goals?

Delineating the Learning Outcomes

Learning outcomes function to direct the unit's actions by providing a lens or focus as the unit engages in the process of education.

These learning outcomes, therefore, establish a framework for subsequent decisions in the unit vis-à-vis what is taught and how it is taught.

Since the only things that can be taught are (a) some knowledge (b) some skill and/or (c) some disposition, then units must delineate the general characteristics for its candidates vis-à-vis what they should know, be able to do and be disposed toward.

Learning outcomes, therefore, describe the characteristics of the way of life the unit envisions for its graduates. These characteristics may also be construed of as **institutional standards** if standards are defined as normative positions of what should be.

To generate learning outcomes, a unit may begin by considering the present realities in professional education and identify teaching and learning characteristics it deems as good. Conversely, the unit may also identify teaching and learning characteristics it deems as not so good. The unit can then project the way of life it sees for its graduates, some five to ten years in advance (i.e., the beliefs and knowledge the candidate should possess, the skills he/she should demonstrate, and thoughts, behaviors and emotional attachments - dispositions - he/she should evince). It is this way of life that should characterize the outcomes for current unit candidates.

John Goodlad, in an interview with Mark Goldberg (2000) maintains that "A leadership training program, ..., should be a 'logical continuation of the best training available to be a teacher" (84). In that case, units may simply extend their learning outcomes for initial level programs to include any unique standards for educational leaders, etc. in advanced programs. The assumption here is that the common focus for teacher, administrator, school counselor, etc. is the enhancement of P-12 student learning.

A unit may solicit confirmation of its learning outcomes from its professional community (the levels of agreement or disagreement with) by developing a survey in which each of the learning outcomes are identified and feedback sought on two dimensions regarding the characteristics that every candidate in the unit should evince in his/her professional life. Members of the unit's professional community might be asked, regarding each outcome, (a) whether current candidate graduates demonstrate the characteristic(s) or outcome(s), and (b) whether candidate graduates ought to demonstrate the characteristic(s) or outcome(s) in his/her professional life.

The unit's activity in delineating learning outcomes should, therefore, permit it to address the following questions:

Are there clearly defined candidate learning outcomes toward which the unit's effort is directed?

Do these educational outcomes facilitate the general knowledge, skills, and dispositions that all graduates should possess?

Can each outcome be captured in a single word or phrase?

Stating the Knowledge Base

For every learning outcome, that is, institutional standard, identified by a unit there should be good reasons or evidence for believing that a candidate's way of life in teaching or other professional roles ought to be that way. The justification offered for particular ways of life in teaching or other professional roles in schools should emerge from the knowledge base on teaching and learning and other professional roles in schools, for example, administration, counseling, and so on. In other words, each learning outcome identified by a unit should be justified as a reasonable way of life in teaching or other professional roles though theoretical knowledge, contemporary research, or the wisdom of practice as delineated in the current knowledge base literature (Murray, 1996; Reynolds, 1989; Wittrock, 1986). This knowledge base enables a unit to justify not only the purpose for having its outcomes, but also the reasons for teaching candidates certain things and in certain ways so that they might come to possess the outcomes and therefore have a greater impact on P-12 student learning.

In other words, gathering knowledge base evidence to justify unit outcomes may be guided by John Stuart Mill's notion regarding (a) method of agreement (b) method of difference and (c) method of concomitant variation. The knowledge base literature should provide the following justification (a) that a particular outcome will occur only if certain methods are used or content provided; (b) that conditions present when the outcome does not occur cannot be sufficient conditions for the occurrence of the outcome, and (c) that the more closely the variations in some content or method are correlated with the variations in an outcome the greater the probability that one produces the other (Copleston, 1966, 75-76).

A measure of continuous improvement in a unit is the degree to which, from time to time, it reexamines its outcomes, and its justification for those outcomes, that is, the knowledge base for the learning outcomes.

The unit's activity in stating its knowledge base should lead to answers to the following questions:

Is each outcome shown in the literature on teacher education and/or other professional roles in schools to be germane to teaching and learning or other professional roles (empirical and/or theoretical knowledge and/or craft wisdom)?

Showing Standards Alignment

According to the National Commission on Teaching and America's Future (1996) "Standards for teaching are the linchpin for transforming current systems of preparation, licensing, certification, and on-going development so that they better support student learning" (67). The commission goes on to suggest:

Clearly, if students are to achieve high standards, we can expect no less from their teachers and other educators. The first priority is reaching agreement on what teachers should know and be able to do in order to help students succeed. Unaddressed for decades, this task has recently been completed by three professional bodies, The National Council for Accreditation of Teacher Education (NCATE), the Interstate New Teachers Assessment and Support Consortium (INTASC), and the National Board for Professional Teaching Standards (The National Board). Their combined efforts to set standards for teacher education, beginning teacher licensing, and advanced certification outline a continuum of teacher development throughout the career. These standards offer the most powerful tools we have for reaching and rejuvenating the soul of the profession (Summary Report, What Matters Most: Teaching for America's Future, September 1996, 18).

The development of professional accountability in teacher education may therefore be seen as a continuum that links a College of Education (a unit) responsible for the initial preparation of candidates, to the public authority for its operation, a State, to the induction process for candidates into the field (school sites), to the professional and learned societies that shape what is taken for knowledge in the respective fields (national societies), to the accomplished professional as judged by the National Board for Professional Teaching Standards (NBPTS).

Quality assurance in teacher education when viewed through a three-legged stool metaphor (NCATE, INTASC, NBPTS), enables Schools/Colleges of Education to be guided by institutional, state, and professional standards, especially if standards are defined in a normative sense as measures of what ought to be. The pursuit to align standards is, therefore, a pursuit to improve the preparation of teachers and other school personnel through standards-based reform. The goal of the reform is enhanced student learning in P-12 settings.

A school/college seeking national accreditation is, therefore, required to lay out its conceptual framework in a manner that "provides a context for aligning professional and state standards with candidate proficiencies expected by the unit and programs for the preparation of educators" (NCATE 2000 Unit Standards, March 31, 2000, 2).

The unit's activity in showing standards alignment must lead to answers to the following questions:

Can the unit learning outcomes be linked to any professional and/or state standards to ensure a quality effectiveness continuum?

Showing Long Term Goals Alignment

The juxtaposition of vision (what we want) and a clear picture of current reality (where we are relative to what we want) generates ... 'creative tension'. Learning in this context does not mean acquiring more information, but expanding the ability to produce results we truly want in life. It is lifelong generative learning (Senge, 1990, 142).

Peter Senge's notion of "creative tension between what ought to be, one's vision or aim, and current organizational realities, what is, produces a needs index for change. This index may be translated through long term goals. Goals, in this context, may therefore be construed as mechanisms for planning for change. They create opportunities for short term successes or failures that fuel the change process. A long-term goal is therefore a general statement regarding what a unit would like to see happen and consequently long-term goals take time to accomplish.

The development of long term goals may emerge through different paths. For example, one goals development path emerges from vision to goals to achieve the vision (Peterson, 1995). Another example of goals development emerges from mission to goals to achieve the mission (many universities engaged in developing performance outcomes use this strategy) .

The option proposed here emerges from the conceptual idea of a unit's long term goals being construed as means through which the unit's vision/theme, mission, and philosophy/aim are advanced.

In other words, the long-term goals become the steps through which evidence to demonstrate progress in a unit's aim is manifested (through plans, goals, objectives, timelines, and use of results for change and improvement). In this option, planning and evaluation (strategic planning) is given meaning through the conceptual framework in terms of what the unit delivers in order to achieve its aim. The goals become an extension of a unit's aim and therefore are not someone else's goals being adopted. Instead, they should reflect the unit's values, and sense of purpose. As noted by Senge (1990) "... nothing happens until there is vision. But it is equally true that a vision with no underlying sense of purpose, [aim] no calling, is just a good idea - all 'sound and fury, signifying nothing'" (149).

It is the identification and pursuit of explicit goals that foster the experimentation, results orientation, and commitment to continuous improvement that characterizes a unit's learning community. Goals, therefore, foster ongoing accountability, and performance benchmarks become natural accountability indicators to measure progress and growth.

To begin the process of goals development a unit may be guided by John Dewey's dictum that "... aims relate always to results" (Dewey, 1944, 101). However, as Dewey so cogently illuminated, the distinction between results and ends is that results follow any "exhibition of energy" while end "possess intrinsic continuity" (Dewey, 1944, 101):

> An aim implies an orderly and ordered activity, one in which the order
> consists in the progressive completing of a process. Given an activity having
> a time span and cumulative growth within the time succession, an aim means
> foresight in advance of the end or possible termination. If bees anticipated the
> consequences of their activity, if they perceived their end in imaginative
> foresight, they would have the primary element in an aim. Hence it is
> nonsense to talk about the aim of education--or any other undertaking--where
> conditions do not permit of foresight of results, and do not stimulate a person
> to look ahead to see what the outcome of a given activity is to be (Dewey,
> 1944, 102).

A unit may use its educational aim as a foreseen end that gives direction to unit activities by aligning its goals with the normative ends contained in the NCATE Standards.

Using the standards as external conditions of what ought to be in the profession, and juxtaposing them against internal unit conditions should produce means (i.e., goals) by and through which the unit may reach its aim.

This discrepancy format thus enables a unit to frame its goals categories through the categories deemed by the profession as critical; for example, the NCATE 2000 Standards would yield the following goals categories: (a) candidate learning performance and unit assessment evaluation systems (b) unit culture vis-à-vis curriculum, candidate and faculty composition (c) faculty performance and (c) unit accountability.

A unit's activity in carving out its long term goals should lead to answers to the follow question:

Can long-term goals (e.g., regarding candidate performance, program assessment and unit evaluation, field experience and clinical practice, unit culture, faculty performance, and unit will and capacity) be derived that are consistent with professional standards of what ought to be to ensure quality effectiveness and be extensions of the unit's vision and mission and in harmony with unit philosophy and educational aim?

Maintaining an Evaluation/Assessment System

The unit's evaluation and assessment systems should be structured conceptually to enable decisions to be made regarding whether the unit is achieving its aim and learning outcomes and therefore producing desired results. Evaluation and assessment must be conceptually constructed to show both elements being essential features of the unit's continuous development.

The conceptual framework as a way of seeing, thinking and being enables units to move from questions of purpose (why) to questions of content (what) to questions of method (how). The "when" of the unit's efforts is its assessment and evaluation system that enables it to ascertain whether its candidates and graduates are acquiring the unit's learning outcomes, and consequently whether the unit is achieving its overall aim, its purpose.

Once a unit has decided upon its purpose for existence, it must next decided what should be taught in its programs to achieve that purpose. Units must ensure the following:

(1) that candidates know the subjects they will teach;

(2) and can demonstrate the knowledge and competence expected of beginning or experienced teachers or other school personnel.

A unit may utilize both internal and external evaluative checks of the foregoing.

On the other hand, the unit's use of a conceptual framework as a way of seeing and thinking facilitates its also seeing and thinking about requisite input processes such as the culture of the unit in terms of candidate and faculty composition and propensity to enrich diversity in the curriculum, etc.; faculty performance and development, that is, their scholarship of the classroom; the institutional and unit will to govern, and capacity to provide necessary resources and facilities.

The conceptual framework, therefore, facilitates evaluation and assessment to be seen and thought about on two levels: the unit and the individual candidate. The unit needs to know whether its graduates are mastering institutional, state and professional standards, and how related enablers such as unit culture, faculty performance, and so on are contributing to such success. The unit also needs to know whether each candidate is learning the content, professional and pedagogical knowledge, skills and dispositions appropriate to his/her field as demonstrated by the individual's performance.

A unit may conceptualize the foregoing accordingly:

1. Be able to offer conceptual justification for why candidate performance is assessed the way it is.

2. Delineate what is assessed? How is it assessed? When is it assessed? Who assesses it? What measures are used to determine validity and reliability of assessments? Who monitors the assessment system?

3. Lay out a timeline for the implementation and operation of the foregoing.

On the other hand, information about the unit's productivity, resources, and personnel is critical to the unit's evaluation of organizational level performance.

The following model captures the essence of the above:

Why is Candidate Performance Assessed the Way it Is?
[Conceptual Framework Justification]

	1	2	3	4	5	6	7
A							
B							
C							
D							
E							
F							
G							

Timeline for Implementation

1. Pre-entry knowledge, skills, and dispositions
2. Content knowledge
3. Professional knowledge, skills, and dispositions
4. Teaching/Professional ability in field and clinical practice (effect on P-12 student learning)
5. On the job performance first year
6. Graduates' perceptions of the program's impact on their performance
7. Enablers to facilitate the above vis-à-vis unit culture (diversity), faculty vitality and production, and unit will and capacity (resources).

A. What is assessed?
B. How is it assessed?
C. When is it assessed?
D. Who assesses it?
E. Are rubrics used to assess? Are the validity and reliability of the rubrics checked?
F. Who monitors the entire evaluation and assessment system?
G. Are results used to improve programs and the unit?

The overall evaluation and assessment system may be captured accordingly:

	Programs	Unit
Internal	Candidate Performance Assessment	Resources Data Productivity Data Personnel Data
External	Candidate Performance on state and national exams	Graduates' Feedback Employers /Clinical Supervisors Evaluation

The unit's activity vis-à-vis its maintaining an evaluation/assessment system must enable it to answer the following questions:

Is there an overall evaluation system in the unit to determine whether graduates are acquiring the unit's learning outcomes?
Does the system provide internal and external checks on candidates' performance?
Does the system provide internal and external unit operational data?
Does the system ensure assessment of goals progress and use of results in the unit's improvement process?
Does the system foster ongoing unit accountability?

The Conceptual Framework and Continuous Improvement

Having a sense of purpose is a catalyst for change. According to Fullan (1993):

> ... personal purpose is the route to *organizational* change. When personal purpose is diminished we see in its place groupthink and a continual stream of fragmented surface, ephemeral innovations. We see in a phrase, the uncritical acceptance of innovation, the more things change, the more they remain the same. When personal purpose is present in numbers it provides the power for deeper change (14).

If one perceives a conceptual framework as engendering a sense of unit purpose, then the more persons in the unit committed to that purpose the greater the power for change. In fact, one may construe the essential activity for keeping a conceptual framework current as inquiry "the engine of vitality and self-renewal" (Pascale, 1990, 14). In other words, the relationship between the conceptual framework (unit purpose) and continuous improvement (inquiry) is "the ability to simultaneously *express and extend* what you value. The genesis of change arises from this dynamic tension" (Fullan, 1993, 15).

Continuous performance improvement is therefore facilitated by the conceptual framework as the aim of the unit is facilitated by a process of continuous improvement that moves from a conceptual big picture to parts and back to the whole to the use of results to effect change.

To improve presupposes a state in which one is becoming. Having some sense of direction for the development and refinement of improvement goals, strategies and measures, enhances one having some degree of coherence. Continuous improvement should therefore be a matter of assessing oneself against standards of what ought to be and developing a needs index for growth.

Continuous improvement should facilitate the unit's way of making meaning of its decision making in how it delivers its curriculum, how it attends to its candidates, how it enhances faculty vitality, and how unit accountability is provided. In this context, the unit's goals planning is given meaning vis-à-vis what is delivered in order to achieve its aim. This goals focused model leads to a relationship between the unit, its departments and programs, and the products and goals each develops in order to enhance a unified, and coherent operation.

The following model may be useful to units as a means to conceptualize continuous improvement:

Continuous Improvement Model

University Mission	Unit Vision/ Mission	Department Mission	Programs

**What ought to be - professional standards - minus what is
In operation: where you want to be minus where you are
Now leads to needs index or goals.**

Goals	Goals	Goals	Goals for Candidate Performance
1.	Candidate Performance	⇔	Knowing that
2.	Unit Evaluation	⇔	Knowing how
3.	Unit Culture	⇔	Effect on P-12 student
4.	Faculty Performance	⇔	learning
5.	Unit Accountability	⇔	

How do we evaluate our success in achieving our aim?

Improvement Goals	Improvement Goals	Improvement Performance Plan
Plan/objectives	Candidate Performance	What is assessed? How is it assessed?
Budget	Evaluation & Assessment System	When is it assessed? By whom is it assessed?
Measures of Success	Culture	Rubrics used (validity, Reliability)
Performance Indicators		Who monitors?

RESULTS UTILIZATION

The Conceptual Framework and Tangible Board of Examiners Evidence

NCATE Board of Examiners (BoE), as part of their on-site visits to colleges of education, must describe a unit's conceptual framework in their reports. The various units therefore become cases that focus the attention of the various members of the BoE on a unit's whole or big picture in a manner that enables BoE members to understand how the big picture or whole is manifested in organizational realities such as teaching, curriculum delivery, candidates' assessment, and so on.
Learning about and seeking on-site evidence for the following conceptual framework indictors should assist BoE members to discover vital underlying connections and interdependencies in a unit. This kind of learning should enable BoE members to "simultaneously ... hold the whole in mind and to investigate the interactions of the component elements of the whole...." (Vaill, 1996). The focus of the BoE members in this endeavor is not simply on how things are being done in a unit (the technical side of things), but instead their focus is on deriving meaning of a unit's endeavors by looking at the purposes to which a unit puts its technical activities and data and the human meanings and relationships in the unit's professional community that is enriched by those activities and data (Vaill, 1996). To understand and be able to describe a unit's conceptual framework BoE members must, therefore, acquire both academic (that documented) and "participatory" knowledge (that captured from on-site participation) of a unit.
For BoE members to gain meaning about a unit's conceptual framework they must avoid a form of reductionism in which different individuals in a unit's professional community are asked to respond to the single infamous question "what is your conceptual framework?" Instead, BoE members must realize that they are trying to understand why the unit thinks, sees, and behaves the way it does. Information gained from each of the following elements should enable the BoE members to craft a written narrative that describes and evaluates the function and utilization of a unit's conceptual framework in providing direction for programs, courses, candidate performance, faculty teaching, research and creative activities, and service, and unit accountability.

Affirming a Shared Vision

NCATE Board of Examiner teams (BoE) must secure a clear understanding of the unit's foreseen end, that is, its desired future if they are to provide a clear description of this indicator of the unit's conceptual framework. Understanding implies some ability to explain, interpret and/or apply. Members of the unit and its professional community should be able, therefore, to demonstrate their understanding of the unit's desired future, and its consistency wth institutional and unit missions, through their explanation, interpretation, and application. The BoE should demonstrate its understanding of the unit's desired future by its explanation of it in the BoE Report.

BoE team members may affirm the existence of the unit's desired future as gleaned from the unit's articulation and explanation of it in documents. However, in order to obtain a deeper understanding of this desired future, the BoE might solicit from unit members their explanation and interpretation of the unit's desired future. Dialogue with unit members (e.g., administrators, faculty, candidates, graduates, school personnel) should reveal the justification for the desired future, and the degree to which it has been shared.

The BoE should frame their dialogue with questions of who, what, when, why, where, and so on. Linda Shadiow of Northern Arizona University, whose materials were shared with BoE trainees in Covington, Kentucky, July 23-28, 2000, suggests that BoE members might elicit useful information in interviews by utilizing (a) process/absence questions - to verify or confirm something (b) inventory questions - to identify multiple ways of the use of something (c) process/clarification questions - to seek amplification on how something is used, and (d) relational/impact-effect questions - to understand the inter-relationships and consequences of something in use.

The BoE in its report on this indicator of the unit's conceptual framework should therefore, as a result of the foregoing, be able to explain the unit's shared vision (or lack thereof) as gleaned from the insightful and credible reasons offered by unit personnel for what the unit wants to become, and what it has been charged to do.

Ascertaining Coherence in Program

After acquiring an understanding of the unit's **shared vision and mission**, the BOE should next look for the following conceptual guide.

The team should turn its attention to looking for the underlying wisdom (that is, philosophy) which influences the conduct of life in the unit as it is intelligently directed by some aim.

According to John Dewey (1916/1944) "... all ancient schools of philosophy were ... organized ways of living, those who accepted their tenets being committed to certain distinctive modes of conduct..." (324). In other words, the BoE is seeking to ascertain whether there is any consistency of response in the unit to the plurality of events, that is, curricular, instructional, clinical, evaluative, administrative, and so on, which occur in and out of the unit, and which have direct bearing on the unit's operation.

The BoE should not be looking here for the facts of the unit. Instead, the BoE must look for "permanent dispositions of action toward life" (Dewey, 1916/1944) in the unit. In other words, the blueprint for the unit's existence; that is, the values and principles upon which the unit's being and doing are based.

What is this unit wisdom? Is it articulated in documents? Is it shared? What is the strength of the grip which this wisdom has upon unit members in pushing them to act for its realization in the unit's curriculum, instruction, field/clinical experiences, assessment and evaluation systems?

Understanding Professional Commitments

The unit's wisdom, that is, philosophy, provides the BoE some sense of that to which the unit is committed, that is, its aim. One means through which the unit furthers the attainment of its aim is the learning objectives for candidates (institutional standards). In other words, what behaviors and attitudes (**outcomes**) must candidates demonstrate in order to achieve the unit's shared vision, mission, philosophy and aim?

The BoE must examine the evidence the unit presents to demonstrate candidate progress in achieving unit aim(s). A prerequisite for the BoE, however, is to understand what the unit is prepared to do regarding candidate learning, and its effect on P-12 student learning. Do the knowledge, skills, and dispositions candidates must demonstrate in order to achieve the unit's vision, mission, and aim include knowledge, skills, and attitudes for helping all students learn and for integrating technology in their instruction?

Are the members of the unit's professional community, in particular the candidates, and faculty, well aware of these outcomes?

Does the unit offer justification that is grounded in empirical, theoretical and/or the wisdom of practice for these outcomes, that is, these knowledge, behaviors, and attitudes expected of candidates?

Checking Standards Alignment

Understanding that to which the unit and its programs are committed, vis-à-vis institutional standards, enables the BoE to compare institutional standards with state and professional standards for teacher education candidates and other school personnel. Does the unit provide any alignment between and among its institutional standards and those of state and professional origin? Does this alignment really enhance what some call a quality assurance mechanism in the preparation of teachers and other school personnel?

Looking at Long-Range Goals Alignment

The other means by which the unit advances its aim is through short and long term goals. The BoE should be interested in gaining some conceptual sense of how steps are taken, timelines projected, and the evidence secured and used to demonstrate unit progress toward its aim.

Judging the Evaluation/Assessment System for Candidate Performance

Can members of the unit's professional community explain, and interpret the connection between the unit's means for judging effectiveness and the achievement of the unit's shared vision, mission, philosophy, and educational aim? How is continuous improvement in candidate learning characterized in the unit? How is unit accountability envisioned?

Summary

A comprehensive description of the above by the BoE in its report (Part II) for initial or continuing accreditation visits should provide a clear picture of the underlying structure or system in the professional education unit that gives conceptual meanings to a unit's operation and provides direction for programs, courses, teaching, candidate performance, faculty scholarship and service, and unit accountability.

This description should facilitate an understanding of how the unit fashions a coherent perspective by relating its parts into a coherent whole. The description should also enable one to understand how the unit's conceptual framework acts as the stimulation of a unit ethos within which continuous improvement, renewal, and change will occur, for initial accreditation seeking institutions and does occur for institutions seeking continuing accreditation.

CHAPTER FOUR

PUTTING IT ALL IN PLACE: A WORKING FRAMEWORK

The following working conceptual framework emerges from my association with Dr. I. Ira Goldenberg, former dean of the college of education at Florida International University, and from my work as NCATE Coordinator for the college during Dean Goldenberg's tenure.

What follows is a working conceptual framework that benefits from a vision/theme articulation by a faculty, the mission formation of a former dean Ira I. Goldenberg, the delineation of underlying philosophical, psychological and pedagogical values, an educational aim, and learning outcomes by the author that were affirmed through a faculty survey, a knowledge base developed by faculty and the author, standards alignment done by the author, a performance assessment and evaluation system crafted by the author, and a continuous improvement and long-term goals model shaped by the author.

While the working conceptual framework will be linked to a mythical unit at Podunk University, the majority of the actual language in the working framework may also be found in documents developed at Florida International University during 1992 and 1999.

The Working Conceptual Framework: Unit Vision/Theme

At Podunk University, the unit's desired future emerged as a result of collaborative dialogue among the faculty and its professional community (content, professional and pedagogical, and P-12 faculty, candidates, and professionals from the world of practice). This vision for the unit is captured in a **theme**, which the unit feels is "an effective means to communicate the essence of a vision and [affords] an easy way for people to remember the vision." The overarching vision/theme for the unit and its programs, both at the initial and advanced preparation levels is to **facilitate learning and change within diverse populations and environments.** This vision/theme, for the unit, is directed by the following understandings of the theme as it applies to the initial and advanced levels:

Facilitator of Learning

Teachers, educational leaders, or related professionals who facilitate learning are <u>knowledgeable about the individual backgrounds, preferences, interests, and learning styles of their students</u> and use this knowledge to assist students to reach their full potential.

Learning

Learning should be directed toward <u>meeting the needs of diverse populations</u>. To do this, program graduates must move beyond their own personal experiences and, as a result, value the experiences of all people. Learning should also be directed toward <u>meeting the needs of a changing environment</u>, both the physical environment of living on a planet whose resources are disappearing and the human environment of an increasingly diverse population. Learning, therefore, is the acquisition of personal meaning rather than simply a measurable outcome.

Change

Educators who are open to new experiences and find <u>continued learning</u> exciting will be able to play a major role in shaping the changes that will occur. Within this context, educators need to <u>have knowledge of technology</u>, science, and the ethical implications of the advances in these areas.

Urban Context

The Unit's vision/theme relates to the urban, multicultural, multi-ethnic community in which the unit is located. The public school district, which the unit serves, is the nation's fourth largest school district. Within the schools, there are children from 139 different nationalities and representative of 163 different languages and dialects. The unit's contiguous school district, the 10th largest in the country, has similar, though less dramatic demographics. In addition, the influx of immigrants from Latin America and the Caribbean is continuing to change whole neighborhoods. Thus the needs of the communities served are changing, and the College must change to meet these needs.

Thus, the unit's desired future is to **"facilitate learning and change within diverse populations and environments**."

<u>Unit Mission</u>

All colleges of education are called upon to fulfill two separate (and often conflicting) mandates. The first is the historical charge to educate and prepare teachers, administrators, and other professionals to function as competent, creative, and knowledgeable facilitators within the different learning environments that exist to serve students and other citizens. The second mandate is broader in nature and includes both the need to discover and disseminate knowledge about the developmental process itself and the need to study, understand, and change the social, economic, and political conditions that restrict the possibilities of learning and development. Taken together, this dual mission <u>demands that a college of education both prepare people to deal effectively with an existing reality and to address itself to the dilemma of changing that reality.</u>

What distinguishes eminent colleges of education is not a difference in mission; it is the ability to serve 'two harsh masters' in a manner that alters public consciousness, fosters public discourse, and influences public policy regarding the role of education in a pluralistic society. To the degree that a college of education is successful in forging a clear and understandable link between its professional preparation and social change functions, to that degree does it build for itself the external recognition reserved for eminent institutions of learning.

... College of Education exists as a professional school in a university that defines its mission as:

- providing educational access and academic/professional excellence, - serving the broader community and enhancing the area's capacity to meet cultural, economic, social, and urban challenges, and

- creating better understanding among the people of the Americas and the world.

The bridge between the College of Education's professional preparation and social change mission must be defined in terms of the broader University's traditional commitment to excellence in teaching, research, and service. It is, however, in the College of Education's understanding of the meaning and implications of 'excellence in teaching, research, and service' that the College develops a special meaning, identity, and sense of itself as an educational community.

A. <u>Teaching</u>

The lifeblood of the College of Education is its students. Mirroring the University's commitment to access and opportunity, they are an extraordinary heterogeneous group: multi-cultural and multi-racial; of varying economic and social backgrounds.

They represent students of both traditional and non traditional age, needs, and aspirations. Their experiences with us will have a profound, perhaps immeasurable, impact on their subsequent effort to help others. If they experience learning as an exciting and validating adventure, they will approach others with a sense of adventure.

If they experience learning as a joyless task that only highlights limitations and reinforces weaknesses, they will approach others with a sense of resignation.

Given the above, the quality of teaching and support that is available to students at the College of Education takes on a very special meaning. Teaching and student support must involve much more than the traditional socializing and processing of mirror images of ourselves.

As faculty in a college of education, we must fulfill (and model) the three separate but related conditions of teaching that warrant the designation of excellence. First, as professors, we must articulate our beliefs in the capacity of people to learn and grow, and we must profess these beliefs openly, with candor, and with conviction. Second, as educators, we must create the conditions and provide the support that is needed to learn and grow. And third, as teachers, we must share our skills, knowledge, attitudes, and values with students in ways that enable them to experience their own competence, creativity, and potential. In the final analysis, teaching is a studied art form, and the faculty of a college of education should not only be better at it than anyone else, it should also help others throughout the University become teachers. This is a measure of distinction.

B. Research

Research is the substantial pursuit, discovery, and dissemination of knowledge. It involves the systematic ordering of data in ways that illuminate the human condition. As such, it is an activity and a process that has critical implications for the College of Education. Most importantly, it provides the College of Education with a powerful and persuasive context through which its efforts to both study and understand the present and to change the future can be shared with its own and other communities.

The College of Education's commitment to the importance of scholarly and rigorous research is not, and should never be, externally driven. It is derived from the internal push to discover and understand the variables and forces that either facilitate or impede the learning process.

Given the complexity of the issues and dynamics that affect learning, research at the College of Education must be multi-dimensional in nature. There is no single approach to the discovery of knowledge that is better or more scientific than any other. There are only different approaches and different methodologies, and the choice of a methodology should be dictated by the problem being studied, not vice versa.

The College of Education embraces the view that basic, applied, and action research are co-equal in importance and status.

Consequently, the willingness and ability to expect, advocate, and   support
varying approaches to the pursuit of truth is a measure of distinction.

C. Service

Service is the process by which a setting engages itself in, and becomes an
integral part of, the environments in which it exists and the people who provide
it with its ultimate source of agency.

The College of Education exists in a geographic area undergoing acute social
change; it exists in a nation that is struggling to discover its common themes;
and it exists in a world that is only beginning to fathom the implications of
inhabiting an ecosystem that is as fragile as it is precious.

The College of Education exists at a time when the consequences of change
and technology have coalesced to underscore the importance of learning at the
very moment when we are confronted with the lingering indictment of whole
groups of people who have been historically under-served or systematically
excluded from the possibilities of education.

Given the above the College of Education is committed to:

- Becoming even more directly engaged in addressing the needs and problems
of urban education through the development of collaborative and reciprocal
relationships with ... County School Systems and other professionally related
communities.

- Utilizing its expertise to develop, implement, and evaluate programs of
national and international significance, programs aimed at building bridges
between people, cultures, and societies.

- Addressing the unmet educational needs and aspirations of historically under-
served populations: the poor, minorities, women, adult learners, the elderly, and
the physically, mentally, and emotionally challenged.

- Developing interdisciplinary programs to address the causes and educational
consequences of poverty, racism, and sexism in a pluralistic society.

- Becoming active participants in the process of shaping and developing public
policy in the areas of education and human welfare (Developed in major part
by I. Ira Goldenberg).

The College of Education cannot and should not refrain from debate. Its
mission, identity, and evolving meaning demand responses that are
conceptually innovative, fiscally sound, and programmatically supportive of a
progressive educational agenda (Written in part by I. Ira Goldenberg, former
dean of the college of education at Florida International University, 1989).

The College of Education at Podunk University approaches its state
and institutional charge, its **mission**, through a three-part mission
statement. The first is to prepare teachers, and other professionals (i.e.,
counselors, administrators, school psychologists, etc.) to function as
contemplative, competent, creative, confident, capable and
knowledgeable facilitators disposed to using technology to facilitate
learning within the different learning and developmental environments.

The second mandate is broader in nature and includes: (1) the need to discover and disseminate knowledge about the developmental process itself; and (2) the need to study, understand and if necessary change the social, economical and political conditions that restrict the possibilities of learning and development.

The third directive focuses on the professional community and the College's role in working with other professionals, within the local, national and international areas and in the professional organizations, to promote educational, social, economic, technological and political change and advancement in relation to educational contexts.

The unit's mission is therefore consistent with its institution's purpose: **The mission of this state University** is to serve the people of Southeast Florida, the state, the nation and the international community by imparting knowledge through excellent teaching,
creating new knowledge through research, and fostering creativity and its expression.

The College of Education's faculty and administration at Podunk University chose to use a way of thinking that moves from its vision/theme and mission to its underlying beliefs embedded in its vision/theme, and mission. The unit could have chosen a way of thinking that moves from a mission to the long-range goals perceived as necessary to achieve a mission.

Instead, the unit at Podunk University ascribes to the idea that it is critical to first understand the underlying beliefs about reality, truth and knowledge, ethics and values which give meaning to the unit's existence and which form the basis for critical decisions regarding the center from which the unit approaches the life of the teacher and other school personnel preparation.

Unit Philosophy

The faculty's analysis of its vision/theme and mission and the major philosophical consensus among its members enables the unit's guiding philosophy to find its grounding in holistic and constructivist paradigms.

As a result, there is an underlying commitment to the following beliefs: (1) the serious problem affecting the modern American educational system reflect a deeper crisis in the culture; and, (2) the dominant cultural values and practices.

For example, the emphasis on competition over cooperation, and bureaucracy over authentic human interaction have been destructive to optimal human development.

The fundamental purpose of education should therefore be to nourish the inherent possibilities of human development. Schools must, therefore, be places that facilitate the learning and whole development of all learners.

Teachers must honor students as unique and valuable individuals. In other words, teachers must welcome personal differences and foster in each student a sense of tolerance, respect, and appreciation for human diversity. Teachers must be facilitators of learning, which is an organic, natural process and not a product that can be turned out on demand. Teachers require the autonomy to design and implement learning environments that are appropriate to the needs of their particular students.

Learning is an active, multi-sensory engagement between an individual and the world, a mutual contact that empowers the learner and reveals the rich meaningfulness of the world. Experience is dynamic and ever growing.

The goal of education must be to nurture natural, healthy growth through experience. Holism and constructivism celebrate and make constructive use of evolving, alternate views of reality and multiple ways of knowing. When educators are open to their own inner being, they invite a co-learning, co-creating process with the learner. Genuine education can only take place in an atmosphere of freedom. Freedom of inquiry, of expression, and of personal growth is all required.

Unit Aim

Given the lens through which the unit sees the world of teaching and learning and other school personnel endeavors - its **aim** - the unit establishes coherence through its conceptual framework by establishing a clearly directed purpose for all unit activity that emerges from its vision/theme, its mission statement, and its underlying values and principles upon which it rests its being and doing.

The unit's **aim "to facilitate education and growth through individual empowerment, interconnectedness and social change"** thus establishes a basis for subsequent decisions about what candidates and other school personnel should know and be able to do: in other words, the unit's commitments to candidate learning and to its goals.

The long-term goals are thus derived as a discrepancy needs index between the commitments delineated in national standards (what ought to be), and the current commitments status in the unit (what is). The unit's long term goals are construed as a means through which the unit's vision/theme, mission, and philosophy are advanced.

That is, the steps to take, for example, goals and objectives, the timelines, and the evidence to demonstrate progress in the unit's aim to facilitate education and growth through individual empowerment, interconnectedness and social change.

The College of Education at Podunk University thus seeks through its vision/theme, and mission to empower professionals by enabling them to acquire knowledge, skills, and dispositions necessary to assume control over their lives. The unit's aim also requires that the College assist professionals to understand that for all our differences, as human beings, we are connected, have common needs and aspirations, can relate to each other in supportive and helpful ways, and can celebrate our diversity. Thus, the College of Education seeks to facilitate change by evoking and supporting in professionals an orientation, awareness and commitment to improving the human condition. In other words, its aim is to facilitate education and growth through individual empowerment, interconnectedness and change.

The unit's aim, that is, its directed purpose, thus provides direction for what should be taught (its curriculum), its delivery of field and clinical experiences, its assessment and evaluation of candidate performance, it evaluation of faculty scholarship (teaching, research and service), and unit accountability, that is, unit will and capacity.

<u>To facilitate education and growth through individual empowerment, interconnectedness and change.</u>

This unit's aim establishes a basis for subsequent decisions about what to teach (the matter of general education, professional education and content studies), and how to teach (the matter of the knowledge base). In other words, the understandings/knowledge, skills and dispositions that form the unit's learning outcomes are shaped by, and lead back to, the unit's aim to facilitate education and growth through individual empowerment, interconnectedness and social change.

Empowerment

The aim to empower denotes individuals having the knowledge, skills, and attitudes necessary to exercise control over their lives. If individuals have knowledge and skills to exercise control over their lives then they may be said to have power.

The knowledge, skills, and attitudes that professional educators need to empower themselves in their control of their professional pedagogical decisions is according to Darling-Hammond, Wise, and Klein (1995): "... transmitted through professional education and by initiation through supervised clinical practice under the guidance of experts" (p. 17).

The Unit empowers its graduates by facilitating their acquisition of (a) content knowledge - the factual information, organizing principles, and central concepts of their disciplines/subjects of study (Grossman, Wilson & Shulman, 1989); (b) pedagogical-content knowledge - the ability to take content knowledge and help others understand it (McDiarmid, Ball & Anderson, 1989); and (c) pedagogical knowledge - knowledge of how to teach.

Interconnectedness

The unit's aim to foster interconnectedness is predicated on the belief that whatever their differences, people have certain common needs and aspirations, and that they can relate to each other in helpful and supportive ways and can celebrate their diversity. According to the Global Alliance for Transforming Education (GATE, 1991):

> ... each of us - whether we realize it or not - is a global citizen... In
> the emerging global community, we are being brought into contact with
> diverse cultures and world views as never before in history .... It is time for
> education to nurture an appreciation for the magnificent diversity of human
> experience....Education in a global age needs to address what is most fully,
> most universally human in the young generation of all cultures (p. 6).

What is most fully and universally human is connectedness and interdependence of nature and human life and culture, the value of cooperation and balance; the needs and rights of participants; human rights; justice; the search for meaning; love; compassion; wisdom; truth; and harmony (Education 2000, 1991).

The unit views its work with professional educators as the mechanism by which this sense of universal human connectedness may be nurtured, and thus enhanced in the broader society.

Change

The unit's aim to enhance social change is driven by the notion that change must be seen as an orientation, awareness and commitment to improving the human condition. Teachers and other professional educators are agents for social and societal transformation. If the ultimate pedagogical aim of education is to foster participatory democracy then the unit's aim to enhance the improvement of the human condition may be extrapolated from the words of Bruce Romanish (1991):

> ... democracy at a minimum speaks to the power of individuals to construct their society and lives along lines compatible with basic values that relate to the dignity and worth of all people. To the extent powerful forces control resources and engage in oppressive actions against the citizenry, one's education should provide the capacities and understandings for collective action. To the extent society contains inequities and injustices one's education should provide the wherewithal for participating in activities that confronts those realities. Democratic education should equip individuals with the experiences and ethical constructs which enhance the creation of democratic communities not only in the political realm but wherever people join together in common ventures and endeavors (p. 40).

The unit, through its aim, therefore affirms another guiding principle in the Vision Statement of the Global Alliance for Transforming Education that:

> The building of a truly democratic society means far more than allowing people to vote for their leaders - it means empowering individuals to take an active part in the affairs of their community. A truly democratic society is more than the 'rule of the majority' - it is a community in which disparate voices are heard and genuine human concerns are addressed. It is a society open to constructive change when social or cultural change is required (Education 2000, 1991, p. 6).

Unit Educational Goals/Outcomes

The theme, the mission, the philosophy, and the aim are all actualized in the stated learning outcomes of the unit, and it is the unit learning outcomes that form the link to the statement of the understandings, skills, and dispositions that form the basis of each program.

The outcomes, or **institutional standards**, of the unit are designed to identify the general knowledge, skills, and dispositions that all graduates of the College of Education at Podunk University as professional educators or other related professionals are expected to possess:

The professional educator in initial preparation programs in the College of Education at Podunk University:

1. Knows the philosophical and historical context of teaching and learning [**CRITICAL THINKER**]
2. Reflects on appropriate practice, (that is, the nature of students, of learning environments, and of strategies for enhancing learning) [**REFLECTIVE PRACTITIONER**]
3. Knows subject matter, curricula, pedagogy, and the educational process [**INSTRUCTIONAL LEADER**]
4. Appreciates the diverse contexts of schools and promotes the acceptance of diversity [**CHANGE AGENT/EDUCATOR RESPONSIVE TO CHANGE**]
5. Develops alternative solutions to educational problems [**PROBLEM SOLVER**]
6. Disposed to professional self-growth [**SELF-DIRECTED PROFESSIONAL**]

Graduate students in the College of Education are expected to assume leadership roles in their chosen fields, whether as teachers, in administration in schools, the community college, college or university, in a supervisory capacity of subject matter areas, or in counseling and psychological services. They are expected to be self-directed individuals who have elected to follow advanced studies in their chosen discipline.

They seek not only national certification and licensing renewal, but scholarly examination of various fields of leadership in education.

Graduate programs are permeated with the spirit of inquiry, reflection and research, tempered by pragmatic needs for career advancement. To this end, candidates are enabled to follow a course of study that, has a core of experiences, but allows for particular content studies designed to enhance and empower the participants.

The professional educator, at the advanced level(s) is *self-directed* by virtue of his/her empowerment as:

1. learner planning and realizing his/her development,
2. teacher with a conscientiously formed and increasing effectiveness in the education
   of children, youth and adults,
3. leader drawing students, families and communities into the common endeavor of
   educating children, and youth, and
4. individual evidently secure in his/her identity, his/her caring for others and him/herself, and his/her quest for greater knowledge and understanding.

The professional educator, who is *reflective* by virtue of essential disciplinary and pedagogical knowledge, analyzes, tests, and applies educational policies and practices in his/her classroom, school, school district, and other educational agencies. The professional educator is *critically minded* by virtue of his/her questioning and continuously improving educational conditions, goals and processes and his/her effectiveness in fulfilling the needs of his/her clientele. The professional educator is a *practitioner* by virtue of his/her primary engagements in actual activities, which affect and realize teaching and learning in schools, districts and other educational agencies.

The professional educator in advanced level preparation programs at Podunk University:

1. Is guided by knowledge of what teaching and learning should be
   [CRITICAL   THINKER   and   SELF-DIRECTED PROFESSIONAL]
2. Is knowledgeable of the nature of students and individuals in schools and other learning environments

[REFLECTIVE PRACTITIONER and INSTRUCTIONAL LEADER]
3. Has a greater understanding of the meaning of social change and its relationship to the everyday life of schools and other educational agencies
[CHANGE AGENT and PROBLEM SOLVER]

Figure
College of Education Professional Education Model
Initial

THEME

Facilitating learning and change within diverse populations and environments

UNIT AIM

To facilitate education and growth through individual, empowerment, interconnectedness and change.

OUTCOMES

Knows the Philosophical Context of Teaching And learning	Knows the strategies for enhancing learning	Knows subject matter and pedagogy	Promotes the acceptance of diversity	Develops solutions to educational problems	Disposed to self-growth

GENERAL EDUCATION

Understandings, Skills and Dispositions
Communicates ideas and concepts in the primary and at least one other language.
Appreciates the important role of mathematical ideas and concepts.
Understands how scientific theories and procedures relate to the world.
Thinks critically about the foundations of thought.
Appreciates life perspectives distinct from his/her own.
Is cognizant of the social nature of humans.
Appreciates the arts.

CONTENT STUDIES

Understandings, Skills and Dispositions

Understands what is taken for knowledge in the field/discipline and the ways that knowledge is organized/structured.

Understands the subject matter in depth and mastery.

Understands the moral and ethical questions related to specific subject matter.

Is able to engage in the pursuit of new knowledge in the field/discipline.

Is disposed to using a variety of methods including technological innovations in the subject to enrich learning.

PROFESSIONAL/PEDAGOGICAL STUDIES

Understandings, Skills and Dispositions

Knows how teaching and learning should be approached from a philosophical perspective.

Knows how to enhance learning.

Knows subject matter and pedagogical principles.

Can develop solutions to educational problems.

Is disposed to change and diversity.

Is disposed to professional growth.

Figure
College of Education Professional Education Model
Advanced

THEME

Facilitating learning and change within diverse populations and environments

UNIT AIM

To facilitate education and growth through individual empowerment, interconnectedness and change

OUTCOMES

Demonstrates insight into The social and philosophical Patterns that shape the form Schooling takes	Demonstrates ability to think about teaching and learning as a reflective practitioner and educational leader	Is disposed to an appreciation of the changing and diverse contexts of schools and communities

CONTENT STUDIES

Understandings, Skills and Dispositions

Understands what is taken for knowledge in the field/discipline.
Understands the subject matter in depth and mastery.
Understands the moral and ethical questions related to specific subject matter.
Is able to engage in the pursuit of new knowledge in the field/discipline.
Is disposed to using a variety of methods including technological innovations in the subject to enrich learning.

PROFESSIONAL/PEDAGOGICAL STUDIES

Understandings, Skills and Dispositions

Is guided by knowledge of what teaching and learning should be.
Is knowledgeable of the nature of students and individuals in schools and other learning environments and of the methods and strategies for enhancing learning.
Has a greater understanding of the meaning of social change.

The foregoing figure(s) specifies the major elements of each initial and advance level program in the unit. For instance, documentation for each program of Content Studies will be the five outcomes listed in the box entitled "content studies" while documentation for each program of Professional and Pedagogical Studies will be based on the box entitled "Professional/Pedagogical Studies." Thus the various programs within the unit have a template for fostering consistency and coherence among the college's theme, mission, philosophy, aim, and outcomes while still demonstrating the uniqueness of each.

The College of Education, at Podunk University, is therefore guided by a conceptual framework that establishes a sense of unity across all the programs in the college. This framework provides a sense of direction for the development and refinement of programs, courses, [teaching], research, and service. It sets forth the operational manner of the college, and establishes goals that will lead to a unified whole while still permitting individual interests and pursuits.

Conceptual Framework as a Way of Being

The college's conceptual framework, therefore, establishes a "way of thinking" or "way of being" that moves from the unit (whole) to its parts (programs, projects, etc.). This "way of thinking" facilitates the college's way of making meaning of its decision activities in terms of:

(1) the curriculum (how the curriculum is delivered), (2) candidates
(how the college attends to candidates), (3) faculty (how the college
enhances faculty vitality) and, (4)   governance (how unit
accountability is provided).

This framework for making meaning thus facilitates movement from
matters of purpose (why), to matters of content (what), to matters of
method (how), to matters of evaluation and assessment (determining
when the purpose has been achieved).   In utilizing a conceptual
framework as a way of seeing, being, and thinking, the unit is able to
give meaning to its activities in terms of what is delivered in order to
achieve its aims.

If one views a conceptual framework as a way of seeing the world
(one's frame of reference), then one, like the unit at Podunk University,
recognizes the necessity of having to articulate underlying beliefs and
values **(philosophy)**.   Since philosophy enables one to explore
questions of existence, then the unit's conceptual framework should
enable it to delineate its reasons for existence **(its aim)**.

Aims give rise to a unit examining why it is preparing its graduates.
As a result, **learning outcomes** should be articulated that enable one to
know what graduates should know **(understandings)**, what they should
be able to do **(skills)**, and to what they should be disposed **(disposed)**.

The Unit's conceptual framework thus leads to a **model** of the
relationship between the unit, its departments, programs, and the
products and goals each develops in order to enhance a unified, and
coherent operation (see model below).

Figure
COE Conceptual Framework Model

Vision/Theme

UNIT (College)   DEPARTMENTS   PROGRAMS

Mission   Mission

WHY

Philosophy   Philosophy   Philosophy
Aim   Aim   Aim
Outcomes   Outcomes   Outcomes

	Knowledge Skills Dispositions		Knowledge Skills Dispositions
	GENERAL STUDIES		C O
WHAT			U
	CONTENT STUDIES		R S
	PROFESSIONAL STUDIES		E S
HOW	....	Delivery	
WHEN	....	Evaluation	

Knowledge Base for Outcomes

The learning outcomes for the unit and its programs at Podunk University are grounded in a knowledge base. In other words, why the respective learning outcomes are important for the unit is justified through the knowledge base literature for teacher education. This literature on teacher education clearly shows that there are recognized knowledge base(s) that should influence the preparation of teachers and teacher educators (Reynolds, 1989; Wittrock, 1986).

Lee Shulman (1987), for example, identified three types of knowledge [bases] necessary for expert teaching:

1. Expert teachers must have **content knowledge**, that is, knowledge of the subject matter to be taught. According to Pamela Grossman et al. (1989), content knowledge refers to "the stuff of a discipline (field of study); factual information, organizing principles, central concepts" (p. 27). These authors maintain that: "an individual who possesses content knowledge of biology [for example] knows about RNA and DNA, about theories of evolution and heredity, about ecosystems and nervous systems" (p. 27).

2. Expert teachers must have **pedagogical-content knowledge**. Pedagogical-content knowledge enables the teacher to take the content knowledge and help others understand it.

3. Expert teachers must have **pedagogical knowledge**, that is, knowledge of the general variety that includes knowledge of how to motivate students, how to manage groups of students in a classroom setting, how to design and administer tests, and so on (Sternberg & Horvath, 1995, p. 11).

On the other hand, the work of Houston (1990) and Murray (1996) clearly highlights a knowledge base for teacher education in general while the work of Jackson (1992) and Wagner (1993) does the same for respective disciplines.

The Unit's /Programs' Knowledge Base

The unit's knowledge base is linked to its six outcomes.   Each outcome is grounded in a knowledge base that is congruent with "best practices."

The key to the programs knowledge base is the link by all programs in the unit to the unit's five (5) content studies outcomes:

Content Studies Outcome #1 (understands what is taken for knowledge in the field, and how that knowledge is organized), and Content Studies Outcome #4 (understands how new knowledge is acquired in the field) enable programs to articulate this **content knowledge** for their respective programs.

Content Studies Outcome #2 (understands the subject matter in depth and mastery), Content Studies Outcome #3 (understands the ethical dimensions in the field), and Content Studies Outcome #5 (is able to use a variety of methods to enhance learning in the field) enable programs to articulate this **pedagogical-content knowledge**.

Programs are able to indicate what the literature in their respective fields say about the best ways to represent the concepts and ideas in the field for candidates' understanding.

The professional and pedagogical studies component in each teacher education program overlap with Content Studies Outcome #5 to assist in the facilitation of **pedagogical knowledge**.   This pedagogical knowledge includes knowledge about learners/learning, about curriculum, educational contexts, educational aims, and general methods.

The following figure captures the link between the unit's aim, outcomes, and knowledge base:

**The Professional Educator as Facilitator of Learning within Diverse
Populations and Environments (Unit Vision/Theme)**
Initial Preparation
Unit Aim   **Outcomes**

To facilitate individual   Knows the philosophical context of
teaching/learning   [critical thinker]
Empowerment,
Interconnectedness and   Knows strategies for enhancing learning
Social change   [reflective practitioner]
                                      Knows subject matter & pedagogy
                                      [instructional leader]
                                      Develops solutions to educational
                                      problems
                                      [problem solver]
                                      Disposed to self growth
                                      [self-directed professional]
                                      Promotes acceptance of diversity
                                      [change agent]

KNOWLEDGE BASE FOR OUTCOMES

Knowledge Base (Initial Programs)

   The Critical Thinker developed by the unit and its programs (1) can
think philosophically, sociologically and historically about classrooms,
schools and other learning environments, about cultural pluralism and
learning, about curriculum planning and design, about educational
professionalism, or about educational governance and can analyze
educational policy and practice (2) can teach for thinking that fosters
intellectual curiosity, open-mindedness, respect for other viewpoints,
and healthy reasoned skepticism (3) is guided by belief systems
reflective of philosophical/historical knowledge of what teaching and
learning should be (4) can create positive learning climates that
promote responsible student behavior (5) knows what is taken for
knowledge in his/her field (6) knows subject matter in depth and
mastery (7) understands the moral/ethical questions related to his/her
content area (8) can engage in the pursuit of new knowledge in the field
(9) can use a variety of methods including technological innovations
(the supporting literature, that is, the empirical, theoretical and wisdom
of practice justification chosen by the unit goes here).

The Reflective Practitioner developed by the College (1) is knowledgeable of the nature of all students and individuals in schools and other learning environments and the methods and strategies for the enhancement of learning and individual growth (2) knows strategies for enhancing learning, i.e., knows the rationale for using certain skills in particular teaching/learning situations (3) knows the fundamental principles of teaching/learning and uses that knowledge to guide his/her actions when confronted with real-world classroom problem and knows how to improve a teaching/learning situation situations to which the principles apply (4) thinks as a professional educator to change it in some constructive way (5) can connect subject matter to pedagogical action (6) can link instruction to technological strategies (the supporting literature - empirical, theoretical and wisdom of practice - goes here).

The Instructional Leader developed by the College (1) can demonstrate subject matter expertise (2) can make the subject meaningful for students (3) is knowledgeable of curriculum development and design (4) has evaluative skill in designing experiences and ordering them to effectively achieve goals of instruction (5) is grounded in curriculum knowledge to meet the needs of emergent society, students, and subject matter (the supporting literature - empirical, theoretical and wisdom of practice - goes here).

The Change Agent developed by the College (1) can create positive learning climates that promote responsible student behavior (2) knows how to help and assist all students especially those having difficulty, those who are under-prepared or those with exceptionalities (3) knows the role of the teacher/professional educator in emphasizing cultural diversity, pluralism and global perspectives (4) knows how to create learning climates that foster respect, relatedness, receptivity and trust (5) can add to the knowledge of his/her field (6) can provide learners multiple paths to new knowledge (the supporting literature - empirical, theoretical and wisdom of practice - goes here).

The Problem Solver developed by the College (1) can analyze educational problems and develop solutions (2) can foster active inquiry (3) can engage in reflective practice (4) can foster relationships with colleagues, parents, and the community (5) can help students enhance their knowledge (gain new insights) of the subject through problem solving (the supporting literature - empirical, theoretical and wisdom of practice - goes here).

The Self-Directed Professional developed by the College (1) can articulate his/her basic values and beliefs (2) can employ critical reflection and seeks the creation of personal meaning after considering a full range of alternative value frameworks and action possibilities (3) values professional interactions (4) knows the relationship between self-directed learning and responsible change (5) can help students examine and understand the ethical dimensions of the content under study (the supporting literature - empirical, theoretical and wisdom of practice - goes here).

The Professional Educator as Facilitator of Learning within Diverse Populations and Environments (Unit Vision/Theme)
Advanced
Unit Aim   **Outcomes**

Unit Aim	Outcomes
To facilitate education and growth through individual empowerment, interconnectedness and social change	Is guided by knowledge of what teaching and learning should be [critical thinker and self directed professional] Is knowledgeable of the nature of students nd individuals in schools, and other learning environments, and of the methods and strategies for the enhancement of learning [reflective practitioner and instructional leader] Has a greater understanding of the meaning of social change and its relationship to the everyday life of schools and other educational agencies [change agent and problem solver]

KNOWLEDGE BASE FOR OUTCOMES

Knowledge Base (Advanced Programs)

The **Critical Thinker/Self-Directed Professional** developed by the College: (1) knows the philosophical, historical, social, political and multicultural contexts in which schooling takes place; (2) knows the interrelationship among learners, teachers, and the social context; (3) can interpret philosophical differences in educational thought;

(4) knows how to engage in reflective inquiry; (5) knows how to examine and shape his/her own professional and curricular values; (6) can employ critical thinking strategies for all learners; (7) knows how to engage in scholarly activities; (8) knows what is taken for knowledge in the field; (9) can help students examine and understand the ethical dimensions of the content under study; (10) knows how to engage in the pursuit of new knowledge in the field. (the supporting literature - empirical, theoretical and wisdom of practice - goes here).

The **Reflective Practitioner/Instructional Leader** developed by the College: (1) understands individual difference in learning performance; (2) knows content and has the ability to facilitate student learning; (3) can manage and monitor student learning; (4) can think systematically about practice and learn from experience; (5) is committed to students and their learning; (6) can use instructional strategies and technologies for diverse student populations; (7) can engage in reflective research inquiry; (8) can strengthen his/her subject-matter base through research, reading, study and collaboration with colleagues (the supporting literature - empirical, theoretical and wisdom of practice - goes here).

The **Change Agent/Problem Solver** developed by the College: (1) knows the social, cultural, political, economic and comparative contexts in which schooling takes place; (2) can influence community political efforts; (3) can critically examine assumptions in a way that leads to conceptual, attitudinal, and value changes; (4) knows how to receive the languages all learners bring to school as opportunities for growth, and shared collaborative learning; (5) knows how to be involved as a member of a learning community; (6) can assume leadership roles within professional organizations. (Supporting literature - empirical, theoretical, and wisdom of practice goes here).

<u>Standards Alignment</u>

Ensuring a quality effectiveness continuum is very important for faculty and its professional community at Podunk University. The development of professional accountability in the preparation of teachers and other school personnel is seen by the unit as a continuum that links the College of Education at Podunk University (a unit) responsible for the initial preparation of candidates to the professional and learned societies that shape what is taken for knowledge in the respective fields; to the public authority for its operation, a State; to the induction process for candidates into the field (school sites); to the new and accomplished professional as judged by the National Board for Professional Teaching Standards.

Quality assurance in the unit becomes a matter of being guided by internal professional standards (**institutional standards**) that are congruent and aligned with **state standards** and **national standards** (Interstate New Teacher and Assessment Consortium Standards, INTASC, and National Board for Professional Teaching Standards).

Since the unit is a part of a quality assurance continuum, its way of seeing and thinking, its conceptual framework, is intended to contribute to the authority which governs its existence, the State, and to the profession, manifested in national subject area societies. As a result, the conceptual framework of the unit at Podunk University, its way of seeing the world, acts as a catalyst in the unit's contribution to the state and the profession.

Having decided the performance learning outcomes vital to achieving its aim, the unit then contributes to the state and national standards by showing that its learning outcomes are compatible with and reinforce the performance learning outcomes of the state and related state organizations such as INTASC who have crafted performance standards for licensing new teachers and national organizations such as NBPTS.

The unit's conceptual framework thus facilitates the unit moving from its performance learning outcomes to reinforcing those performance outcomes promulgated by state and national bodies.

Unit Outcomes		INTASC Principles	State Standards	National Board Standards
Learning Objectives		Learning Objectives	Learning Objectives	Learning Objectives
Knowledge Skills Dispositions		Knowledge Skills Dispositions	Knowledge Skills Dispositions	Knowledge Skills Dispositions
Program Outcomes	National Program Standards	Subject Standards	Subject Standards	Subject Standards
Knowledge Skills Dispositions	Knowledge Skills Dispositions	Knowledge Skills Dispositions	Knowledge Skills Dispositions	Knowledge Skills Dispositions

The following tables lay out the unit's outcomes (its institutional standards), and show the alignment of those standards with state and national standards. For specific program by program alignment see individual program folios. For specific knowledge, skills and dispositions outlined in each set of standards see attachment(s).

INITIAL PREPARATION ALIGNMENT

Unit Outcome	State Standards	INTASC Principles	National Board Standards
Critical Thinker	#4 Critical thinking #6 Ethics	#4 Plans instruction	#3 Manages and monitors student learning
Unit Outcome	State Standards	INTASC	National Board Standards
Reflective Practitioner	#1 Assessment #7 Development and learning #8 Knowledge #9 Environment #10 Planning #12 Technology	#1 Understands discipline; creates learning experiences #2 Knows about Development #3 Plans #4 Plans #5 Plans #9 Reflects	#1 Knows about Learning
Unit Outcome	State Standards	INTASC	National Board Standards
Instructional Leader	#8 Knowledge #10 Planning #12 Technology	#1 Understands discipline; create learning experiences #7 Plans #8 Knows how to assess	#2 Knows how to teach subject.

Unit Outcome	State Standards	INTASC	National Board Standards
Change Agent	#5 Diversity #9 Learning #10 Planning	#3 Plans #5 Plans #7 Plans	#3 Manages and monitors student learning

Unit Outcome	State Standards	INTASC Principles	National Board Standards
Problem Solver	#2 Communicate well #3 Improvement #11 Role of the teacher	#6 Plans #9 Reflects #10 Collaborates	#4 Thinks about practice; learns from experience #5 Is a member of a learning community

Unit Outcome	State Standards	INTASC Principles	National Board Standards
Self-directed Professional	#2 Communicate well #3 Improvement #11 Role of the teacher	#6 Plans #9 Reflects #10 Collaborates	#4 Thinks about practice; learns from experience #5 Is a member of a learning community

ADVANCED PREPARATION ALIGNMENT

Unit Outcome	National Board Standards	State Standards	INTASC Principles
Critical Thinker and Self-directed Professional	#2 Knowledge of content and curriculum #4 Respect for diversity #5 Instructional resources #6 Meaningful applications of knowledge	#2 Effective communication #3 Continuous improvement #4 Critical thinking #6 Ethics #8 Knowledge of subject matter #11 Role of educator	#1 Knowledge of subject matter #4 Multiple instructional strategies #6 Effective communication #9 Professional commitment and responsibility #10 Partnerships
Unit Outcome	National Board Standards	State Standards	INTASC Principles
Reflective Practitioner and Instructional Leader	#1 Knowledge of students #2 Knowledge of content and of curriculum #3 Environment #7 Multiple paths to knowledge #8 Assessment #10 Reflection	#1 Assessment #7 Development and learning #8 Knowledge of subject matter #9 Environment #10 Planning #12 Technology	#1 Knowledge of subject #2 Knowledge of development and learning #3 Can adapt instruction to individual needs #4 Strategies for individual needs #5 Classroom motivation and management skills #7 Planning skill #8 Assessment of student learning #9 Professional commitment and responsibility

Unit Outcome	National Board Standards	State Standards	INTASC Principles
Change Agent and Problem Solver	#4 Respect for diversity #9 Link to family #11 Professional contributions	#2 Communicate well #3 Improvement #5 Diversity #9 Environment #10 Planning #11 Role of the teacher	#3 Can adapt instruction to individual needs #5 Classroom motivation and management skills #7 Planning #9 Commitment /responsibility #10 Partnerships

LONG TERM GOALS ALIGNMENT

The unit's mission is to fulfill its aim through commitments to learning outcomes for candidates in its programs, and through long-term goals that enhance the unit's unique sense of mission and values. At Podunk University, the following goals' process is utilized. Using the standards in the profession as external conditions of what ought to be vis-à-vis candidate performance, field experiences and clinical practice, commitments to diversity and the use of technology, faculty vitality, and unit will and capacity, the unit then examines its current internal conditions vis-à-vis these areas and identifies long-term goals, the achievement of which will facilitate change in the unit's conceptual framework (in vision, mission, philosophy, aim, and so on). To be effective, this goals process describes:

1. What is to be accomplished,
2. Steps to achieve the goals (objectives),
3. Individual and/or group responsibilities for initiating and/or sustaining each step toward achieving the goals,
4. Timelines for each phase of goals activity, and
5. Criteria to be used in evaluating progress toward the goals.

The unit at Podunk University, in order to advance its shared vision, mission, philosophy and aim pursues long-term goals in the areas of candidate performance, assessment and evaluation of learning, field/clinical practice, faculty vitality, and unit accountability. Unit effectiveness is therefore determined by a process that moves from:

(1) vision/theme, mission, philosophy and educational aim to
(2) goals development and their review to
(3) action plans to implement and evaluate goals activities to
(4) utilizing the results from goals outcomes to effect improvements
and change.

The conceptual framework should provide the unit a useful way of visualizing the elements of candidate performance in content knowledge, pedagogical content knowledge, professional and pedagogical knowledge, skills and dispositions, and effect on P-12 student learning.

CONCEPTUAL FRAMEWORK GOALS LINK

The unit aim is to:	
Facilitate education and growth through individual empowerment	**Unit Means through Candidate Knowledge** Candidates in teacher education and other school personnel programs acquire the content, pedagogical content, and professional knowledge, skills and dispositions necessary to enable them to exercise control of their professional practice
Facilitate education and growth through interconnectedness	**Unit Means through Candidates as a Community of Learners** Candidates in teacher education and other school personnel programs recognize their common needs and aspirations, can relate to learners in P-12 setting in supportive ways (technologically, etc.) and can celebrate and value diversity
Facilitate education and growth through change	**Unit Means through an Assessment and Evaluation System for Candidates** The system that provides candidates with the orientation, awareness, and commitment to improving their professional practice and P-12 student learning.

In the area of candidate performance and assessment and evaluation, the unit seeks to:

(a) **empower** candidates in its programs through the knowledge, skills and dispositions necessary for them to exercise control of their professional practice. These knowledge, skills and dispositions are transmitted through the unit's professional education programs (general education, content and professional education studies) and in the initiation to the world of practice through supervised clinical practice under the guidance of expert professionals;

(b) (b) **foster interconnectedness** by getting candidates in teacher education and other school personnel programs to recognize their common needs and aspirations and to relate to P-12 learners in supportive ways (technologically, etc.) and to celebrate and value diversity;

(c) (c) **promote change** through a program assessment and unit evaluation system that provides candidates with the orientation, awareness and commitment to improving their professional practice and performance and P-12 student learning.

The unit's achievement of its goals in candidate performance should lead to unit graduates being critical thinkers, reflective practitioners, instructional leaders, change agents, problem solvers and self-directed professionals.

In the area of faculty vitality, the unit seeks to: (a) **empower** faculty in its teaching candidates to acquire the knowledge, skills and dispositions necessary to exercise control over their professional lives; (b) **encourage interconnectedness** by promoting through faculty service the idea of relating to others in helpful and supportive ways; and (c) having its faculty **commit to improving the human condition, that is, to change,** through its research and creative activities.

The following figure displays the conceptual connection:

CONCEPTUAL FRAMEWORK GOALS LINK

The unit's aim is to:	
Facilitate education and growth through individual empowerment	**Unit Means through Faculty Teaching** Faculty share their knowledge, skills, attitudes and values with candidates in ways that enable candidates to experience their own competence, creativity, and potential, and therefore exercise control over their professional lives in the classroom or in other school personnel roles.
Facilitate education and growth through interconnectedness	**Unit Means through Faculty Service** Faculty relate to others in helpful and supportive ways, and are active participants in the process of shaping and developing public policy in the areas of education and human welfare.
Facilitate education and growth through change	**Unit Means through Faculty Research and Creative Activity** The faculty's commitment to the importance of scholarly and rigorous research is not externally driven but instead is derived from the internal push to discover and understand the variables and forces that either facilitate or impede the learning process and consequently, the disposition to improve the human condition.

The unit's achievement of its goals vis-à-vis faculty performance should engender democratic growth in the unit's professional community through the faculty's community action to facilitate learning and change within diverse populations and environments.

In the area of unit accountability, the unit seeks to: (a) provide the necessary leadership and resources (i.e., personnel and resource development) to enhance the knowledge, skills and dispositions needed by members of the unit's professional community to be effective human beings and professionals--to **support empowerment**; (b) **facilitate interconnectedness** through a participative form of governance that engenders communication among members, moves the community to action, and works toward the attainment of the unit's aim; and (c) stimulate organizational renewal, that is, **engage in change processes** by continually elucidating the unit's vision/theme, mission, etc., finding resources to help the unit achieve its aim, solving problems, and helping individuals to achieve their personal goals.

CONCEPTUAL FRAMEWORK GOALS LINK

The unit's aim is to:	
Facilitate education and growth through individual empowerment	**Unit Means through Personnel and Resource Development** The unit helps its personnel to be effective professionals by using the tools of administration to assist personnel to acquire the knowledge, skills and dispositions necessary to exercise control over their organizational lives.
Facilitate education and growth through interconnectedness	**Unit Means through Participative Management** The unit fosters through its governance system communication among and between members of the community, moves the community to action, and gets the community to work toward the unit's aim.
Facilitate education and growth through change	**Unit Means though Organizational Renewal** The leadership elucidates the unit's vision, mission, aim and outcomes; secures resources for achieving the unit's aim and outcomes; and helps personnel solve problems.

The unit's achievement of its goals in the area of unit accountability should lead to the creation and continued development of a professional community that is committed to democratic organizational growth.

To pursue its goals the unit utilizes the following strategic goals process to determine unit effectiveness:

1. An analysis of external conditions (that is, normative professional expectations built into the NCATE Standards, the standards of the regional accrediting body, and state standards).

2. The identification of a set of unit long-range goals that are compatible with the unit's aim to facilitate empowerment, interconnectedness and change and external professional expectations.

3. The identification by the unit's programs and departments of current operational realities and the short-term goals needed to correct discrepancies between professional external expectations and current operational realities.

4. The articulation of the steps to achieve the goals (objectives, activities, measures of success, performance criteria).

5. The identification of individuals/groups responsible for initiating/sustaining the steps toward achieving the short-term goals.

6. The identification of timelines for the activities and budget necessities.

7. The identification of the criteria to be used in evaluating progress toward the short-term goals.

8. The identification of the governance group(s) responsible for using the results of the short-term goals activity to effect unit and program changes and improvements.

The unit at Podunk University is therefore using the conceptual and procedural direction provided in the foregoing process to pursue the achievement of its educational aim "to facilitate education and growth through individual empowerment, interconnectedness and change":

Long-term Goal: To enhance the performance of all candidates.

Short-term Goal: Enhance curriculum delivery, candidate performance and unit assessment and evaluation system.

Objectives/activities:

a. To increase the use of technology in all programs.
b. To develop and implement outcomes for all programs.
c. To improve the monitoring and assessing of candidate progress.
d. To engage in ongoing systematic evaluation to determine how well the unit is achieving its outcomes.
e. To institute processes and procedures for entry to the College of Education.

f. To provide candidates at both the initial and advanced levels with an integrated sequence of field/clinical experiences in professional and pedagogical studies and content studies.

g. To enhance and expand the emphasis on multicultural, intercultural, diversity, global and environmental education.

h. To create incentives and structures for recruiting and retaining a diverse student body.

i. To increase college intra- and inter-departmental collaboration.

j. To enhance collaborative program development between the College of Education and the College of Arts and Sciences.

k. To enhance the articulation link between the college and contiguous community colleges.

l. To enhance the college's general education offering.

m. To increase collaboration with practicing professionals.

n. To enhance the placement of all graduates.

o. To provide support to student organizations in the college.

Long-term Goal: To enhance faculty performance as a means to enhance candidates' performance.
Short-term Goal: To enhance faculty professional development.
Objectives/activities:

a. To increase computer technological support for faculty teaching, research and service.

b. To enhance faculty professional development and growth.

c. To increase faculty scholarship achievement.

d. To increase faculty involvement in the world of practice.

Long-term Goal: To provide the necessary leadership to facilitate the enhancement of both faculty and candidates' performance..
Short-term Goal: To enhance unit accountability.
Objectives/activities:

a. To facilitate programs coordination through the unit's conceptual framework.

b. To enhance the unit's communication and decision-making through the unit's decision making and advisory bodies.

c. To develop and evaluate long-range plans consistent with the unit's conceptual framework.

d. To increase faculty commensurate with the unit's vision, mission and aim.

e.   To increase support staff commensurate with the unit's vision, mission and aim.

f.   To enhance appropriate office, classroom, laboratory space to support teaching, research and service.

Unit/Program Evaluation and Assessment System

The professional education unit at Podunk University moves conceptually from questions of purpose (why), to questions of content (what), to questions of delivery (how). Consequently, its evaluation system is conceptually structured to ascertaining whether graduates are acquiring the unit's learning outcomes, and as a result, whether the unit is achieving its overall aim. Questions regarding evaluation and assessment are thus conceptually interpreted as providing answers to how and when the unit is achieving its aim. The unit's aim is **to facilitate education and growth through individual empowerment, interconnectedness and change**. This aim is operationalized through six outcomes:

Teacher educators and other related professionals in the Unit will:
- know the philosophical context of teaching and learning
- know the strategies for enhancing learning.
- know subject matter and pedagogy.
- promote acceptance of diversity.
- develop solutions to educational problems.
- be disposed to self-growth.

Therefore evaluation in the College is construed as a process for determining the extent to which the aim, and outcomes as conceptually developed and organized, are actually producing the desired results.

The College's process of evaluation enables it to: (1) identify the strength and weaknesses of its conceptual plans, and (2) determine the areas in which the curriculum is effective and in need of improvement.

Evaluation is seen, therefore, as an essential feature of the continuous development of the professional education program at Podunk University. This goal attainment model of evaluation is supported in the literature (Bosler, 1989; Brown 1988; Cameron, 1980; Campbell, 1977; and Guild 1990). While Hannan and Freeman (1977) point out several difficulties with the goal attainment model, Seybert (1990) shows that the model is very useful in helping to assess [Unit] effectiveness.

According to Seybert (1990) unit effectiveness is linked to the degree to which educational outcomes are being achieved. Alfred's (1989) model of internal and external assessment variables provides a useful scaffold for the Unit's evaluation measures at the initial and advanced levels. Alfred's two-tier approach presents two major types of assessment activities: those that address candidate learning (i.e., performance), and those that deal with institutional and policy level issues.

The Unit's evaluation framework, as shown in the following Matrix, utilizes a similar two-tier approach except that one tier addresses internal and external checks on program candidate learning (candidate performance) and the other addresses internal and external Unit operational data:

Evaluation: Initial and Advanced Levels

	Program	Unit
Internal	Candidate Performance • Courses • Field/clinical settings	Productivity • Enrollment • FTE's • Years to Degree • Degrees Awarded • Graduation rates • Recruitment and Retention • Diversity • Faculty Characteristics • Faculty Performance
External	Candidate Performance • State Examinations • Rehire Possibility	Graduates Perceptions Employer Evaluation of Graduates Evaluation of Interns

The unit's evaluation process thus enables it to determine whether the curriculum as designed, developed, and implemented is producing or can produce the desired results. The results in question are the unit's aim of empowering people through their acquisition of understandings, skills and dispositions; fostering interconnectedness through experiences in diversity and facilitating change through opportunities for innovative action and service.

Evaluation, at Podunk University, serves, therefore, to identify the strengths and weaknesses of the curriculum before implementation and the effectiveness of its delivery regarding whether to accept, change, or eliminate something.

Involvement of Professional Community

The College is committed to supporting the active and meaningful participation of its professional community in evaluative and assessment decisions that directly impact the continuous improvement of its programs. The following describe how various members of this professional community participate:

1. Unit faculty in initial and advanced programs provides internal evaluative assessment of candidates' performance progress toward Unit and program outcomes.
2. Field-based practitioners provide on-the-job assessment of candidates' application of the skills and understandings learned in the programs.
3. Graduates of the unit's programs, at both the initial and advanced levels provide
   feedback regarding their perceptions of their preparation in the unit's programs.
4. Employers of graduates have the opportunity to provide feedback related to the graduates' performance on the job.
5. Decisions about the use of these data are made collaboratively by the various elements of the unit's governance system. As a result, the professional community is engaged in helping the unit renew effective programs for the preparation of school personnel. The unit's professional community includes not only unit faculty, but also educators in P-12 settings, practitioners who supervise internships and field experiences and participate on advisory boards to the unit, professors for the subject matter content and teacher education candidates.

Assessment of Candidate Performance (Initial)

Assessment and evaluation of candidate performance at the initial level is conducted through the candidate's professional portfolio. This portfolio contains the kinds of assessment products/artifacts that will provide evidence of the candidates knowing the content they will teach.

This content knowledge includes (knowing that) and their being able to teach that content (knowing how).

At the initial preparation level the portfolio development begins in Phase IA of the Unit's curriculum phased delivery system. In this pre-admission to teacher education phase candidates are required to show their potential for success through predictive standardized tests, and grade point averages. In addition, they must show their experience with technology, diversity, children/adolescents/young adults or classrooms; and provide a writing sample through an essay about "what it means to be a teacher."

Candidates in initial preparation alternate master's programs begin their portfolio development in what is Phase IB.

In Phase IB (what is the purpose of education?) candidates' level of proficiency is judged by artifacts of evidence contained in the portfolio through the use of holistic rubrics, and through interviews. These analytical and holistic rubrics determine the candidates' level of proficiency to: foster active inquiry and thinking in student learning; think philosophically and historically about educational matters; analyze educational policy and practice; justify teaching choices; use subject knowledge to help students make procedural and conceptual understanding; enhance learning for students with limited English proficiency. Small teams made up of a cross section of members of the unit's professional community (faculty, school personnel, and Arts and Science faculty) conduct interviews with candidates to affirm their proficiency vis-à-vis unit outcomes.

Mid-point assessment examines candidates' proficiencies (portfolio artifacts and interview) in Phases II and III. In Phase II (how do all people learn?) candidates are assessed on their proficiency to: create positive learning climates; use student individual differences to improve learning; help students acquire second language knowledge and skills; adapt content to students with learning difficulties; use evaluation skills in designing learning experiences; engage in reflective pedagogical inquiry; develop students' cognitive capacity; introduce new knowledge to students; draw on knowledge of human development, subject matter and students to make decisions about teaching practices.

In Phase III (what curricular and pedagogical skills should a professional educator possess?) candidates are assessed on their proficiency to:

link instruction to curriculum through technological strategies; use the subject to organize learning for students; engage students in cultural/intercultural problem solving; provide multiple paths to new knowledge; and use technology to ensure disciplined learning environments.

Exit assessment focuses on Phase IVA and IVB of the Unit's curriculum delivery system. In Phase IVA (does the school as a social institution serve or constrain our ideals of the educated person?) candidates are assessed on their proficiency to: deliver content to students with limited English proficiency and exceptionalities; use knowledge of social, cultural, global, multicultural, and legal aspects of schooling to improve learning; use knowledge of social and cultural theories to explain schooling phenomena.

In Phase IVB (student teaching/internship) (what are the best ways to facilitate exchange of knowledge and experience in the field/clinical settings) candidates are assessed on their proficiency to: develop students' critical thinking; vary the instructional process relative to student needs; use multimedia and other technologies to enhance student learning; demonstrate effective classroom management; use assessments and knowledge of student development to enhance learning in the subject; use self-evaluation strategies for continuous improvement; collaborate with colleagues and parents to enhance student learning; show subject matter mastery.

Assessment of Candidate Performance (Advanced)

Assessment and evaluation of candidate performance will be conducted through the candidate's professional portfolio. This portfolio will contain the kinds of assessment products/artifacts that will provide evidence of the candidates' spirit of inquiry in knowing the content they will teach or must use (knowing that) and their being able to teach that content or apply it to appropriate settings (knowing how).

The portfolio development will begin in Phase I of the Unit's curriculum phased delivery system. In Phase I the candidates' professional spirit of inquiry will be guided by their constructing meaning as they explore the essential questions "how should professional education be approached?" "Is it an ethical enterprise?" "What should be the aims/purposes of professional education?" The candidates' level of proficiency will be judged by artifacts of evidence contained in the portfolio and by holistic rubrics.

These analytical and holistic rubrics will determine the candidates' level of proficiency to: examine and justify educational policy proposals, arrangements and practices with an aim to understanding - the philosophical, social, cultural, and political approaches to schooling in the United States and other countries; interpret philosophical differences in educational thought; engage in reflective inquiry; employ critical thinking strategies for all learners; engage in the pursuit of new knowledge in the field; understand the structures of the discipline; examine the ethical dimensions of the content under study; strengthen his/her subject matter base through research, study and collaboration with colleagues; and critically examine assumptions in the field in a manner that leads to conceptual, attitudinal, and value changes.

Mid-point assessment will examine candidates' proficiencies in Phases II and III. In Phase II candidates will explore "how do people learn?" They will be assessed on their proficiency to: understand the interrelationship among learners, teachers, and the social context of education; understand what is taken for knowledge in their field; facilitate student learning through content knowledge; manage and monitor student learning; use instructional strategies and technologies for diverse student populations; be involved as members of a learning community; use the languages all learners bring to school as opportunities for growth, and shared collaborative learning.

In Phase III candidates will pursue "what inquiry/research skills should a professional educator possess?" They will be assessed on their proficiency to: examine and shape their own professional and curricular values; engage in scholarly activity; garner new knowledge in the field; understand individual differences in learning and performance; think systematically about their practice and learn from experience; use instructional strategies and technologies for diverse populations; engage in reflective research inquiry; assess student performance in his/her subject; influence community political efforts vis-à-vis decreasing prejudice and enhancing tolerance.

Exit assessment will focus on Phase IV of the Unit's curriculum delivery system. In Phase IV candidates will focus on "what is the best clinical experience(s) that contributes to the professional development of advanced/professional educators?" They will be assessed on their proficiency to: examine and shape their own professional and curricular values; employ critical thinking strategies for all students; using what is taken for knowledge in his/her field; engage in scholarly activities; engage in reflective inquiry.

In addition, they will be assessed on their ability to enhance the interrelationships among learners, teachers, and the social contexts of education; use knowledge of the subject content to facilitate student learning; be committed to students and their learning; use instructional strategies and technologies for diverse student populations; strengthen his/her subject matter base through research, reading, study and collaboration with colleagues; be involved as a member of a learning community; and assume leadership roles within professional organizations.

Conceptual Framework Link to Curriculum Delivery

Phases	Outcome	Field/Clinical	Commitments	Content
Introduction to the field Phase IA	Awareness of expected professionalism; learners, pedagogy and diversity; and use of technology	Observations	Diversity Technology	Introduction to education and General Content Requisites
Phase IB	What is the purpose of education?	Field/clinical observations	Diversity Technology	Philosophical, Historical Foundations and Content Studies
Phase II	How do all people learn?	Field, Simulations, Clinical observations	Diversity Technology Exceptionalities	Psychological Foundations and Content Studies
Phase III	What curricular and pedagogical skills should a professional educator possess?	Clinical	Multicultural Exceptionalities Technology Assessment Research	Effective Practice and Content Studies
Phase IVA	Does the school as a social institution serve or constrain our ideals of the educated person?	Observations Field	Multicultural	Social, cultural foundations, educational policy and school law
Phase IVB	What are the best ways to facilitate exchange of knowledge and experience in the field	Clinical	Multicultural Exceptionalities Technology Assessment	Application of content, professional and pedagogical knowledge, skills and dispositions

While the introduction to the field would not be germane to the programs in the advanced level, there would be an analogous link to phase IB and phase II.

On the other hand, the outcome for phase III would be "what inquiry/research skills should a professional educator possess?"and for phase IV "what is the best clinical experience(s) that contributes to the professional development of advanced professional educators?"

Summary

So is there an underlying structure or system in the unit at Podunk University that gives conceptual meanings to the unit's operations? Is there an underlying structure or system that provides direction for programs, courses, teaching, candidate performance, faculty, scholarship and service, and unit accountability? Do these conceptual meanings facilitate the fashioning of a coherent perspective into the unit at Podunk University by relating its parts into a coherent whole? Does this framework act as the stimulation of a unit ethos within which continuous improvement, renewal, and change can occur?

BIBLIOGRAPHY

Alfred, R.L. (1989, October). Improving institutional stature: Implications, imperatives, and idioms for researchers. Paper presented at the MidAmerican Association for Institutional Research conference, Kansas City, MO.

Arends, R. & Winitzky, N. (1996). Program structures and learning to teach. In F. B. Murray (Ed.). *The teacher educator's handbook: Building a knowledge base for the preparation of teachers.* San Francisco: Jossey-Bass.

Block, P. (1987). *The empowered manager.* San Francisco, CA: Jossey-Bass.

Bosler, S. (1989). *Holistic goal attainment to increase levels of self-help. Teacher's guide and learner's manual.* Indiana: Lafayette Adult Reading Academy.

Brown, M.K. (1988, May). Developing and implementing a process for the review of nonacademic units. Paper presented at the annual forum of the Association for Institutional Research, Phoenix, Arizona.

Buchmann, M. & Floden, R.E. (1992). Coherence, the rebel angel. *Educational Researcher*, 21(9), 5-9.

Cameron, K.S. (1980, Autumn). Critical questions in assessing organizational effectiveness. *Organizational Dynamics*, 9, 66-80.

Campbell, J.P. (1977). On the nature of organizational effectiveness. In P.S. Goodman & J.M. Pennings. *New perspective on organizational effectiveness.* San Francisco: Jossey-Bass.

Colton, A.B. and Sparks-Langer, G.M. (1993, January-February). A conceptual framework to guide the development of teacher reflection and decision making. *Journal of Teacher Education*, 44(1), 45-54.

Cooley, N. and Hitch, E. (1993, Spring). The role of dynamic models in teacher education. *Action in Teacher Education*, XV(1), 22-28.

Copleston, F. (1966). *A history of philosophy:Volume VIII: Modern philosophy.* New York: Image Books.

Covey, S. (1989). *The seven habits of highly effective people: Restoring the character ethic.* New York: Fireside.

Darling-Hammond, L., Wise, A.E., and Klein, S.P. (1995). *A license to teach: Building a profession for 21st century schools.* Boulder, CO: Westview Press.

Dewey, J. (1944). *Democracy and education: An introduction to the philosophy of education.* New York: The Free Press.

Dill, D.D. et al. (1990). *What teachers need to know: The knowledge, skills, and values essential to good teaching.* San Francisco: Jossey-Bass.

Doherty, W.J., Kouneski, E.F. and Erickson, M.F. (1996). Responsible fathering: An overview and conceptual framework. A report prepared for the Administration for Children and Families and the Office of the Assistant Secretary for Planning and Evaluation of the U.S. Department of Health & Human Services under contract HHS-100-93-0012 to the Lewin Group. On-line, retrieved 1/11/2000 at **http://aspe.os.dhhs.gov/fathers/concept.htm.**

Donmoyer, R. (1996). The concept of a knowledge base. In Frank B. Murray (Ed.). *The teacher educator's handbook: Building a knowledge base for the preparation of teachers.* San Francisco: Jossey-Bass.

DuFour, R. and Eaker, R. (1998). Professional learning communities at work: Best practices for enhancing student achievement. Alexandria, Virginia: Association for Supervision and Curriculum Development.

Fenstermacher, G.D. (1994, November-December). Controlling quality and creating community: Separate purposes for separate organizations. *Journal of Teacher Education,* 45(5), 329-336.

Fitzgibbons, R. (1981). *Making educational decisions: An introduction to philosophy of education.* New York: Harcourt Brace Jovanovich.

Fullan, M. (1993). *Changing forces: Probing the depths of educational reform.* London: The Falmer Press.

Galluzzo, G.R. and Pankratz, R.S. (1990, September-October). Five attributes of a teacher education program knowledge base. *Journal of Teacher Education,* 41(4), 7-14.

Gideonse, H.D. (1993, October). Appointments with ourselves: a faculty argument for NCATE. *Phi Delta Kappan,* 75(2), 174-177.

Gideonse, H.D. (1992). The redesign of NCATE 1980 to 1986. In H.D. Gideonse (Ed.), *Teacher education policy: Narratives, stories and cases.* Albany, NY: State University of New York Press.

Gideonse, H.D. (1986). Guiding images for teaching and teacher education. In T.J. Lasley (Ed.). *The dynamics of change in teacher education,* Vol. 1: Background papers from the National Commission for Excellence in Teacher Education. Washington, D.C.: AACTE.

Goldberg, M.F. (2000, September). Leadership for change: An interview with John Goodlad. *Phi Delta Kappan,* 82(1), 82-85.

Grossman, P.L., Wilson, S.M., and Shulman, L.S. (1989). Teachers of substance: Subject matter knowledge for teaching. In M.C. Reynolds

(Ed.). *Knowledge base for the beginning teacher.* Elmsford, NY: Pergamon Press.

Grossman, P.L., Smagorinsky, P. and Valencia, S. (1999). Appropriating conceptual and pedagogical tools for teaching English: A conceptual framework for studying professional development. Resources in Education. ERIC Document Reproduction Service No. ED 431-198. Washington, D.C.: Clearinghouse on Teacher Education.

Grow-Maienza, J. (1996). Philosophical and structural perspectives in teacher education. In Frank B. Murray (Ed.). *The teacher educator's handbook: Building a knowledge base for the preparation of teachers.* San Francisco: Jossey-Bass.

Grow-Maienza, J. (1991). Teacher education and the role of external actors: Four case studies. Paper presented at annual meeting of the American Educational Research Association, Chicago.

Grow-Maienza, J. (1990). Doing or being done to: The complexities and realities of a new MAE program. Paper presented at annual meeting of the American Association of Colleges of Teacher Education, Chicago.

Guild, P.A. (1990, March/April). Goal-oriented evaluation as program management tool. *American Journal of Health Promotion*, 4(4), 296-301.

Hannan, M.T. & Freeman, J. (1977). Obstacles to comparative studies. In P.S. Goodman, J.M. Pennings and Associates. *New perspectives on organizational effectiveness.* San Francisco: Jossey-Bass.

Houston, W.R. (Ed.). (1990). *Handbook of research on teacher education.* New York: Macmillan.

Howey, K.R. and Zimpher, N.L. (1989). *Profiles of preservice teacher education: Inquiry into the nature of programs.* Albany: State University of New York Press.

Jackson, P. (Ed.). (1992). *Handbook of research on curriculum.* New York: Macmillan.

Koppich, J.E. & Knapp, M.S. (1998, April). Federal research investment and the improvement of teaching 1980-1997. Seattle, WA: Center for the Study of Teaching & Policy.

McDiarmid, G.W., Ball, D.L., and Anderson, C.R. (1989). Why staying one chapter ahead doesn't really work: Subject-specific pedagogy. In M.C. Reynolds (Ed.). *Knowledge base for the beginning teacher.* Elmsford, NY: Pergamon Press.

Murray, F.B. (Ed.). (1996). *The teacher educator's handbook: Building a knowledge base for the preparation of teachers.* San Francisco: Jossey-Bass.

Nanus, B. (1992). *Visionary leadership.* San Francisco: Jossey-Bass.

National Commission on Teaching and America's Future. (1996). *What matters most: Teaching for America's future.* New York: Author.

National Council for Accreditation of Teacher Education (1996). Handbook for continuing accreditation visits. Washington, D.C.: NCATE.

National Council for Accreditation of Teacher Education (2000). Draft NCATE 2000 Standards. Washington, D.C: NCATE.

National Council for Accreditation of Teacher Education (1992). *Standards, procedures, and policies for the accreditation of professional education units.* Washington, D.C.: NCATE.

National Council for Accreditation of Teacher Education (2000). Revised preconditions and documentation. On-line, retrieved 5/27/2000 from **http://www.ncate.org/accred/precon.htm.**

Page, E.H., Griffith, S.P. and Rother, S.L. (1998). Providing conceptual framework support for distributed web-based simulation within the high level architecture. Proceedings of SPIE: Enabling technologies for simulation science II, 287-292. Orlando, Florida, 13-17 April 1998. On-line, retrieved 1/12/2000 at **http://ms.ie.org/page/papers/spie/paper.html.**

Pascale, P. (1990). *Managing on the edge.* New York: Touchstone.

Peterson, M. (1995). Harnessing the power of vision. Ten steps to creating a strategic vision and action plan for your community. Preparing your community for the 21st century series. Resources inEducation. ERIC Document Reproduction Service No. ED 383-824.

Plymouth State College (2000). The conceptual framework for teacher education. On-line, retrieved 1/11/2000 at **http://www.plymouth.edu/psc/teach_ed/concept.html**

Reynolds, M.C. (Ed.). (1989). *Knowledge base for the beginning teacher.* Oxford: The Pergamom Press.

Senge, P., Ross, R., Smith, B., Roberts, C., & Kleiner, A. (1994). *The fifth discipline fieldbook: Strategies and tools for building a learning organization.* New York: Doubleday.

Senge, P. (1990). *The fifth discipline: The art and practice of the learning organization.* New York: Doubleday Currency.

Seybert, J.A. (1990, April). Assessment of college outcomes: Student educational goal attainment. Paper presented at the annual meeting of the American Educational Research Association, Boston.

Shulman, L.S. (1987). Knowledge and teaching: Foundations of a new reform. *Harvard Educational Review*, 57(1), 1-22.

Stengel, B.S. & Tom, A. (1996). Changes and choices in teaching methods. In F.B. Murray (Ed.). *The teacher educator's handbook: Building a knowledge base for the preparation of teachers*. San Francisco: Jossey-Bass.

Vaill, P. B. (1996). *Learning as a way of being: Strategies for survival in a world of permanent white water*. San Francisco: Jossey-Bass.

Wagner, S. (Ed.). (1993). *Research ideas for the classroom*. New York: Macmillan.

Wittrock, M.C. (Ed.). (1986*). The handbook of research on teaching*, 3rd edition. New York: Macmillan Publishing Company.

Zeichner, K.M. (1983). Alternative paradigms of teacher education. *Journal of Teacher Education*, 34(3), 3-9.

AUTHOR'S BIOGRAPHICAL SKETCH

The author is a 1976 Miami University of Ohio, Ph.D. graduate. He is currently a member of the Department of Educational Foundations and Professional Studies at Florida International University, Miami, Florida. His teaching responsibilities include undergraduate and graduate courses in social foundations of education.

He has been a member of the American Educational Studies Association for some 22 years, assuming leadership roles for that association with the Committee on Academic Standards and Accreditation, and the association's Executive Council. He was the inaugural President of the Florida Foundations of Education and Policy Studies Society, and has served as an officer of the Southeast Philosophy of Education Society. He is currently President of the Council of Learned Societies in Education, and serves as a member of the National Council for Accreditation of Teacher Education (NCATE) Board of Examiners and the NCATE Unit Accreditation Board. He was an active member of the Unit Accreditation Board's NCATE 2000 Standards Committee, the committee responsible for writing the NCATE 2000 Standards.

His research interest is in the area of humanistic/holistic education. His articles have appeared in the *Florida Journal of Teacher Education, Teacher Education Quarterly, College Student Journal, Educational Foundations Journal, Journal of Humanistic Education* and *Holistic Education* (now *Encounter: Education for Meaning and Social Justice*).

He has edited, *The Forum,* and co-authored *Thinking About Education: Philosophical Issues and Perspectives, Teaching as Enhancing Human Effectiveness,* and *Enhancing Effective Thinking and Problem Solving for Pre-Service Candidates and In-Service Professionals.* His book reviews have appeared in *Choice, Educational Studies Journal, Journal for Students Placed at Risk,* and the *Journal of Negro Education.*